Kan Topeka, Hattie Horner Louthan

Collection of Kansas Poetry

Kan Topeka, Hattie Horner Louthan

Collection of Kansas Poetry

ISBN/EAN: 9783337217969

Printed in Europe, USA, Canada, Australia, Japan

Cover: Foto ©Thomas Meinert / pixelio.de

More available books at **www.hansebooks.com**

COLLECTION

OF

KANSAS POETRY.

COMPILED BY

MISS HATTIE HORNER.

WITH INTRODUCTION BY MR. GEO. R. PECK.

PUBLISHED AS A PREMIUM FOR

THE KANSAS JOURNAL OF LITERATURE, POLITICS, SOCIETY AND ART.

TOPEKA, KANSAS.

1891.

INDEX TO AUTHORS.

INTRODUCTION.

Though the crops of last year were not all that we wished in this region, there is abundant hope in the bright spring days when this little book goes forth to its fate. Kansas has resumed her smile; and is happy, after her trustful fashion, in the loving promises of the season. She has always had literary aspirations, and not a few of her citizens believe that the new Athens, if ever a new one is builded, will be somewhere within her borders. And now, though unusually busy with her plowing and planting, she will, I doubt not, turn aside for a moment to receive this tribute of verse, conscious that she deserves all that can be said in her praise. Kansas is herself a poem; a great, heroic, stormy epic, in which is told a story of more than Homeric grandeur. And it is this that makes us most proud to be her children. Her fields and flocks are pleasant to look upon, and her walls of corn are a better protection to our people than gates of iron; yet it is for something better than these that we give to Kansas our second-best love.

"The light of high communings on thee lies."

This line of Arthur Graves Canfield—which by the way is one that Wordsworth has hardly surpassed—reveals the secret. In the midst of our town building and our railroad building, our reaping and our failing to reap, we have not forgotten the things of the spirit and the riches that dwell therein. All the while some voice has been singing, not always, perhaps, in tune, and striving hard to put into our common lives a cadence, now and then, of that harmony which fills the world. Whatever may appear on the surface, Kansas is as true as ever to her early ideals. Men will not soon forget the days when she gave the world to know for certain that she would not suffer shackles to be put upon her own limbs nor on those of any human being upon her soil. The very soul of poetry was in that struggle; and it is not strange that from that day to this her people, if not always gifted with "the vision and the faculty divine," have certainly not been "wanting the accomplishment of verse." And thus we have gone along building up a State, guiding the potential energies of a new civilization, giving the unused sod to the wooing of sun and cloud, and counting our gains in store and our gains yet to be gathered. Of our material progress, never before equaled, the world has heard something. We have not kept it secret, nor failed frequently to remind the dwellers in less-favored lands of our incomparable soil, climate and productions. But, after all, have we not always understood that these are not the best nor the truest rewards? Have we not often uttered the indignant self-inquiry:

> "Shall we be lured by these things? Are not we
> A something more than mouth and eyes and ears,
> To eat and look and listen life away?"

It is only by asking ourselves these questions, and by asking them rigorously and earnestly, that we can attain to a true view of life. Whatever is best in human nature is appealed to by poetry. The sense of the beautiful, "the joy of elevated thoughts," the mysterious influence of music which neither science nor philosophy can explain, are in the truest sense *valuable.* It is not the possession of the reasoning faculty that most distinguishes man from the brute, but the possession of the æsthetic sense; and it is this that contributes most to his happiness. Great as is the debt we owe to science, it is my belief that the world could better spare a Newton, a Herschel, a Morse or an Edison, nay, it could better give them all up, than to have blotted from its annals the name of William Shakespeare. Nor is it true that the world is outgrowing the need of poetry. On the contrary, now more than ever before is its influence useful and desirable. Matthew Arnold truly says: "More and more mankind will discover that we have to turn to poetry, to interpret life for us, to console us, to sustain us." It may indeed be true that the times are not propitious for the production of high-grade poetry. The great poets who made the first half of the century illustrious are gone; Browning is gone; and the pen that wrote "In Memoriam" writes now no more. And yet, poetry will not die, nor the hunger for it go out of the human heart. The fashion of this world passeth away; but some things endure, because they are grounded in the very souls of men. We need not mourn a lost art, nor imagine that no more songs will be sung and no more poems be written because the world seems to be on its knees to Mammon. Let us be patient. Somewhere, perhaps even now, some finely-attuned spirit is waiting the hour, waiting the opportunity, to give assurance that the race of poets is not extinct.

Meanwhile, in keeping alive the holy fire, Kansas will do her share. She will be represented on Mount Parnassus as she is at the World's Fair—by the voluntary contributions of her citizens. I dare say this little volume is not destined to immortality. But there is good poetry in it—some very good, and some that is, perhaps, more commendable for the spirit that prompted the author to write than for the manner in which the promptings of the spirit were executed. It is not for me to criticise, but to be thankful that so good a collection of Kansas verses has been made. At a time when his neighbors in Topeka are giving so many anxious thoughts to the attainment of that long-felt want, a dam across the Kaw, Mr. Frost deserves thanks for perceiving that, whether its unstable waters are brought into subjection or not, the public will welcome an offering that appeals to a higher instinct than mere material profit. Dams, warehouses, gristmills and elevators are possible everywhere, but who has heard of a Missouri or an Indiana or a Nebraska volume of poetry? This modest book, small, shrinking and unpretentious, is an answer — a sufficient answer, I think — to the loud and vulgar clamor of those who think that all the wisdom of the ages has been exhausted in the making of what we call practical men. I do not doubt that the silver question, and the gold question, and the tariff question are important; what I insist upon is, that the world most needs men who feel the influence of intangible things, of thoughts, of sympathies, and of aspirations that are not put into legislative acts nor encouraged by a vote of municipal bonds. I shall never forgive Noble Prentis for that Manhattan address, when he advised the students of the Agricultural College that it is more profitable to raise onions than marigolds. I could pardon a millionaire for such a sentiment, but him, whose every harvest is one of golden flowers; who has made us all happy by showing how much more precious are beautiful thoughts than bank accounts; him I cannot excuse. All Kansas would applaud a punishment for his delinquency that should condemn him to go on to the end of life's afternoon writing poetry — for everything he writes *is* poetry — to make us wiser and better and happier. I have forgotten how much it was that Milton received for the copyright of "Paradise Lost," but, as everyone knows, it was an insignificant sum. And yet he had his reward. Every poet, great or small, who sings a true song is the beneficiary of his own effort. When William Cullen Bryant found that he could not succeed in the practice of the law, destiny, always rich in compensations, put it into his heart to write "Thanatopsis," and the world, as well as himself, was the richer for the exchange. This volume, imperfect of course, is yet an effort, a striving, if I may use the word, toward better things than those that habitually engage our time and our interest. It represents Kansas as truly as does the Agricultural Department at the State House; perhaps more truly, for wheat and corn are subject to the vicissitudes of the seasons, while poetry takes no heed of hot south winds, and could no doubt find a text in a grasshopper for such a reflection as came to Burns when he turned up the mouse in her nest with his plough:

> "I doubt na, whyles, but thou may thieve;
> What then? poor beastie, thou maun live."

Poetry is wider than philosophy, its functions higher, and its rewards more consolatory and enduring. "Happy is the land that poets love" is a well-worn saying but a very true one, and measured by this test surely Kansas should be well content. Nearly every writer in this volume has had something to say of her beauty, her noble history, her courage, her sunshine or her storms. Let us hope that the day will be long coming that shall silence the praises or quench the devotion of these Kansas singers.

Something I should like to say of music, which is the twin sister of poetry. Only as it is musical is any written language poetical; and it is true always of the greatest of all arts, that the rhythm must be joined to the thought in true and natural harmony. This does not mean that the words must be metrically arranged, nor that the lines must scan, according to the fixed rules of composition; but music must be in them, must pervade them, must redeem and elevate them, or they are not poetry. The Book of Job is a poem; the writings of Edmund Burke, Milton's great plea for "The Liberty of Unlicensed Printing" and much of the prose of De Quincey and Ruskin are, save only in name, poems. On the other hand, of course, there is in the world a vast amount of stuff which has only a sing-song movement to justify its claim to be considered poetry. Perfection in the poetic art requires that the thought and the expression of the thought, the sense and the sound, should be adapted to each other, should move along together, should be, in every line like

> "Two streams that run with equal murmur to the sea."

To what extent this little volume conforms to such a requirement is left to the kindly judgment of its readers. The poems here printed are not the ambitious efforts of veterans but the recreations of amateurs. They have sung "but as the linnets sing," idly perhaps, but yet not without hope. It is an inspiring sign—a sign that life in these busy days has not lost all the value it once held—when men and women can turn from the wearisome routine which is their daily habit, to the fresher fields, the fairer landscapes, the slopes and heights which only a few have the courage to seek. Let us be thankful for the few.

GEORGE R. PECK.

May 4th, 1891.

Ellen Palmer Allerton.

WHO IS TO BLAME?

Two at the altar; oh! fair and sweet
Is the bride, all in white from head to feet.

O'er braids of gold falls the filmy veil
Like a delicate mist, transparent, pale.

On her clear young brow no shadow lies;
There is solemn joy in her shining eyes.

Men gaze with delight, but soberly say,
"She will shirk no sacrifice, come what may.

"She will pray, poor child, as the years go on,
'Nothing for me, Lord, but all for John.'"

What of the bridegroom? Firm of lip,
Heavy of jaw, and sturdy of grip;

Black brows jutting, eyes keen and dark;
"A man," say they, "who will make his mark."

The years go on. But a single aim
Does life hold for him: he toils for fame.

With strain of nerve and with struggle sore,—
Debt over head, and the wolf at the door.

For fame (the laggard, how slow it comes!)
Willing to burrow in squalid slums—

To shiver in attics,—if, by and by,
He may fill a place in the public eye.

Little children creep to his knees,
To be spurned away. Not such as these,

With their pleading faces and voices sweet,
Must bar his pathway or clog his feet.

And the wife? The soft, sweet eyes grow dim,
While he toils for fame, and she—for him.

For him, and for his: small, winsome things
With soft white fingers and silken strings,

Pull her, and rule her, and hold her in thrall—
A willing slave—at their beck and call.

She loves her children, she worships John;
For these gives all. Is it wisely done?

Gone is her beauty. The locks of gold,
Faded and lusterless, thinly fold

Over a forehead all seamed with care;
Her face, once rounded, and smooth, and fair,

Is pinched and hollow, and worn and thin,
And the dimples are gone from cheek and chin.

What has she learned, these dark years through?
Bearing a load that was meant for two.

Has her mind grown broad and her vision wide?
Is the woman wiser than was the bride?

This she has learned, and but little more,
Save household tasks, wrought o'er and o'er:

She has learned that girlhood's hopes are dust;
She has learned the taste of poverty's crust.

The years go on, and there comes a day
When the struggling student is crown'd with bay;

When gracious Fortune—so niggard before—
Lauds him with honors, and gold in store.

On far-blowing winds, over ocean's tide,
The name of a genius is wafted wide.

It is his; and the heart of the wife beats fast
With pride and joy—"He has won at last!"

Joy soon to perish. A sickening fear
Lays its clutch on her heart. She sheds no tear,

But waits and watches. Oh, sorrowful fate!
Worse than the crust or the empty grate.

She has learned at last all the bitter truth—
This woman, robbed of beauty and youth—

More wretched, poor soul, in her mansion fair,
Than ever in attic with rafters bare.

Want she has known, with hunger and cold,
But these were as naught to the pangs untold—

The billows of pain that her bosom stir,
Since John—her John—is ashamed of her.

He wears—at what cost!—his wreath of fame.
A wrong has been done here. Who is to blame?

WALLS OF CORN.

Smiling and beautiful, heaven's dome
Bends softly over our prairie home.

But the wide, wide lands, that stretched away
Before my eyes in the days of May,

The rolling prairie's billowy swell,
Breezy upland and the timbered dell,

Stately mansion and hut forlorn,
All are hidden by walls of corn.

All the wide world is narrowed down
To walls of corn, now sere and brown.

What do they hold, these walls of corn,
Whose banners toss on the breeze of morn?

He who questions may soon be told:
A great State's wealth these walls enfold.

No sentinels guard these walls of corn,
Never is sounded the warder's horn,

Yet the pillars are hung with gleaming gold
Left all unbarred, tho' thieves are bold.

Clothes and food for the toiling poor,
Wealth to heap at the rich man's door;

Meat for the healthy, and balm for him
Who moans and tosses in chamber dim;

Shoes for the barefooted; pearls to twine
In the scented tresses of ladies fine;

Things of use for the lowly cot,
Where (bless the corn!) want cometh not;

Luxuries rare for the mansion grand,
Gifts of a rich and fertile land —

All these things, and so many more
It would fill a book to name them o'er,

Are hid and held in these walls of corn,
Whose banners toss on the breeze of morn.

Where do they stand, these walls of corn,
Whose banners toss on the breeze of morn?

Open the atlas, conned by rule,
In the olden days of the district school:

Point to the rich and bounteous land
That yields such fruit to the toiler's hand.

"Treeless desert" they called it then,
Haunted by beasts and forsook by men.

Little they knew what wealth untold
Lay hid where the desolate prairies rolled.

Who would have dared, with brush or pen,
As this land is now, to paint it then?

And how would the wise ones have laughed in scorn,
Had prophet foretold these walls of corn,
Whose banners toss in the breeze of morn!

BEAUTIFUL THINGS.

BEAUTIFUL faces are those that wear—
It matters little if dark or fair—
Whole-souled honesty printed there.

Beautiful eyes are those that show,
Like crystal panes where hearth-fires glow,
Beautiful thoughts that burn below.

Beautiful lips are those whose words
Leap from the heart, like songs of birds,
Yet whose utterance prudence girds.

Beautiful hands are those that do
Work that is earnest and brave and true,
Moment by moment, the long day through.

Beautiful feet are those that go
On kindly ministries, to and fro—
Down lowliest ways, if God wills it so.

Beautiful shoulders are those that bear
Ceaseless burdens of homely care
With patient grace, and with daily prayer.

Beautiful lives are those that bless—
Silent rivers of happiness,
Whose hidden fountain but few may guess.

Beautiful twilight, at set of sun;
Beautiful goal, with race well won;
Beautiful rest, with work well done.

Beautiful graves, where grasses creep,
Where brown leaves fall, where drifts lie deep,
Over worn out hands—oh, beautiful sleep!

But words are flames; once given vent and space,
  The fiery tide fast overleaps its shore,
And seldom ebbs again into its place.

—*Allerton.*

Who builds above the clouds must dwell alone;
I count good fellowship above a throne.

—*Allerton.*

J. W. D. Anderson.

COMPENSATION.

WITH weary feet the prophet climbs the hill
  O'erlooking the fair land of Palestine.
His eyes, unsatisfied, feast on each rill
  Or fertile plain, or palm tree's silvery sheen.
He may not enter, though his inmost soul
  Perish with longing for the promised land;
The beauteous vision fades, as o'er him roll
  The burial clods, piled by Jehovah's hand.

For fifteen centuries Judea lay,
  Her thousand hilltops glistening in the sun,
Until Mount Sinai's scepter passed away
  And Bethlehem's star proclaimed all nations one.
Now, on Mount Hermon's brow, a group we see
  With garments whiter than the driven snow,
And Moses walks, with step untrammeled, free,
  The land at which he gazed so long ago.

Blest consummation! So to all will come
  The answer to the longings of the heart—
Peace for our strivings, speech for lips now dumb,
  And tears of joy for tears of pain that start;
If not in this life, then in life eternal;
  If not in this world, then on heavenly shore;
Our spirits cannot miss the bliss supernal;
  God lives, is just, and will be evermore.

THE MOUNT OF VISION.

(Class Poem. Class of '89, Baker University.)

Before us loomed the towering Mount of Vision;
  We stood together at the very base,
And, looking upward, made the firm decision
  We'd test the rough ascent with even pace.
We saw the beetling crags and deep recesses
  O'er which our way must lie, but we were told
That he who to the highest summit presses
  Will see the gates to Elysian fields unfold.

Hand joined in hand, we climbed the lofty mountain,
  We passed the jutting crags and threatening peaks;
No pleasant grove was there, nor cooling fountain,
  Nor rest, save that which high ambition seeks.

Yet sweet companionship made labor lighter,
  And obstacles surmounted trained the feet
For fresh exertions, and the way grew brighter,
  Illumed by light that shone from Victory's seat.

We stand together on the Mount of Vision,
  And now we know the path our feet have trod
Has led to Duty's fields, not fields Elysian,
  And far above us stretch the heights of God.
But toward those regions pure we turn our faces,
  O comrades! May our life-work, just begun,
Though other hopes the hand of Time erases,
  Receive at last the Master's word: "Well done."

ONUS VITÆ.

How hard it presses on work-weary shoulder,
  How heavy lies upon thought-laden mind!
  The sigh, the groan, the scalding tears that blind,
The passions that within the heart's deep smoulder —
Like melted lava once, but now grown colder —
  Remembered scoffs and taunts and words unkind,
  Yea, even joys, that passed and left behind
Debris, within our being's core to moulder.

But then, there comes a time by Fate bespoken,
A time that brings the surety of release.
No more will flesh be racked and hearts be broken,
All feeling, whether joy or pain, shall cease:
The burden 's lifted, but is it the token
Of blest Nirvana, or of conscious peace?

Mary L. Bard.

EASE AND CARE.

God's angel counseled me one day
  Sweet peace to make 'twixt Ease and Care;
He bade me have them cast away
  Old feuds, and henceforth be a loving pair.

For Ease soft maiden was, and Care
  A warrior grim, and clad in mail;
His look distressed the tender fair,
  His rough caresses made her pale.

Then having met most oft with Care,
  "Thou art, O friend, of too stern mien,"
I said; "to win yon maiden fair,
  Thou must thine armor doff, I ween."

And unto Ease I said, "O Ease,
  Forget thyself, and do thy best
For others' good—strive thou to please
  Sad hearts, for so is God's behest.

Thus much I said, and stepped aside—
  Then there they met, and wooed and loved,
And in due time Care won his bride,
  And softly down the years they moved.

And through the years there came to birth
  Sweet children, unto whom was given
The boon of doing good on earth,
  And making smooth the road to heaven!

THE MORNING SUNLIGHT.

I stood in the path of the sunlight,
  As the angel opened the gate,
And bade the imprisoned glory
  No more in the courts to wait.

Then forth leaped the tide of sunlight,
  Such a molten, golden wave,

I fancied the angel's footsteps
  Had worn off the golden pave;
And that God had bidden an angel
  To gather the flecks of gold,
And dissolve them there in the sunlight,
  That mortals might thus behold
A gleam of the golden glory
  That gleameth forever and aye,
'Neath the trees, by the crystal fountains,
  Where eternal sunbeams play.

THE NEW YEAR.

Good deeds and ill, dear Lord,
In this fair book shall be;
  And smiles and tears,
  And hopes and fears,
Thy holy eyes shall see!

And many a page, dear Lord,
That only Thou canst read:
  Creation's groans—
  The secret moans
Of hearts that inly bleed.

Look Thou in love, dear Lord;
Help Thou weak hands to write
  'Gainst deeds of ruth
  Strong words of truth —
Strong words of love and light!

Amanda Lowman Bartholomew.

MY MOTHER.

A SIMPLE parsonage — plain and brown —
Where ivies rambled up and down
With sweet-brier roses.
A place the earliest sunbeams kissed,
Nor left till shadowed by the mist
The night uncloses.

'T was here she wrought with patient care
A life whose incense filled the air
With gladness only;
Here heard her call to enter rest,
And left the home a broken nest,
Bereft and lonely.

To children's hearts, and hearts grown strong
With anguish, 't is a lesson long,
And sad the learning:

That prayers nor tears can e'er restore
The loved ones drifted to that shore
    Beyond returning.

We 've learned farewell oft through these years;
She — welcome — where there are no tears,
    But joys supernal.
And closely fold earth's loos'ning bands
Within the house not made with hands,
    Secure, eternal.

O mother, with the soft brown eyes!
In thy fair home beyond the skies,
    Am I expected?
Canst thou not tell me that at last,
When 'cross that threshold all have passed,
    I shall not be rejected?

AT THE RIVER.

(My peace I give unto you. John xiv: 27.)

The river 's not wide,
And the other side
Seems nearer than ever before;
The waves once so dark
Recede from the bark,
As I list for the dip of the oar.

I shudder no more,
For the plash of the oar
Falls in rhythmical cadence so sweet,
It seems but a part
Of the peace in my heart,
As the water flows nearer my feet.

Nor yet do I shrink,
Tho', close to the brink,
The breath from the river grows chill;
For thro' the deep roll
His voice in my soul
Bids the waves and all fears be still.

In the fast ebbing sand,
Uplifted I stand
By a Hand pierced for me long ago;
My sins all confessed,
On His bosom I rest,
He will bear me safe over, I know.

MORNING GLORIES.

BIRTHDAY.

E. R. N.

THESE tuneful bells, all trembling yet
With wealth of heaven's own dew,
This birthday morn, my dear sweet friend,
Began their life for you.

Kissed by Aurora's rosy lips,
They woke with songs of praise
To Him who keeps and blesses you,
Through all earth's winding ways.

As from the flower, down falls the seed
Upon the waiting earth,
And lives again in fragrant bloom
Of beauty's priceless worth;—

So, in my heart, your own true love
Lives now in flowerful story,
And with my own lies folded in
This tell-tale Morning Glory.

Carl Brann.

TO A CHRISTIAN LADY.

My soul in thine; thy soul in mine;
  Our hearts a unity, a tie;
One thought, one soul, one wish, one mind;—
  For I am thou, and thou art I.

And yet, I thou? Can that be so?
  Am I so pure, clean as a dove?
Ah me! My heart much sin doth know;
  'T is stained; but white 's that of my love.

A heart hath evil and hath good:
  Thou art the good; the evil, I:
Thou giv'st the heart its holy mood,
  But I the sins that in it lie.

And still we are one soul, by rood!
 Thou does me good; uphelp'st me thou;—
The bad is swallowed in the good;
 For I, in thee, art only thou!

MULTUM EX PARVULO.

A LITTLE light so dimly shone
 That hardly was the dark dispelled;
But, far away, a traveler lone
 Its flickering, dying flame beheld.
Discouraged, 'neath revolting sky,
O'ercome by storm, about to die,
The faint red ray renewed his heart,—
 He toiled anew, and found a way;
That humble spark in humble part
 Still driving forth its lurid ray.

So, from the humblest human heart,
 Some lambent beam—faint, lonely ray—
May fall on one, and hope impart
 That gives that soul eternal day;
For souls live not themselves alone,
But intershine for laugh or groan;
Each liquid ray, through joy profane,
 May penetrate some darkened haunt,
Where aching hearts, with racking pain,
 Are dying for the hope they want.

TO MY HEART.

LIFE is not a heavy load,
Need is not a cruel goad;
A lighted plain, a fragrant path,
Dripping of the sacred blood
From the skies, a spirit flood,
A laughing heart, the soul man hath.

Pain? A grief? A galling care?
Canst thou not a sorrow bear?
From that white throne of grace above,
Union with thy pain is sought,
Smiles from thee with blood are bought;
Uplifting, woe-relenting love!

Fainting heart of worldly life,
Lift those brows above the strife;
Uprise with joy, expanding soul;
Virtue's grace and Purity's smile
Woes from out thy deep beguile,—
An ocean of the light doth roll.

—Sad and melancholy heart,
Pleasures are but pains in part;
The smiles bring tears, kind words are hard,
Warmth is heat, the heart doth sink,
Light and pain doth ever link:
O Heaven, God, this death retard!

Those who have no reverie,
Lightsome, laughing, and so free!
—But why should'st thou e'er envy those?
God is good, and Heaven pure,
Sunlight in good hearts is sure,—
Ah, life is light! and God's smile grows!

Arthur Graves Canfield.

MY FAITH.

Be not an anchor, O my faith, to lie
  On ocean's slimy floor, dim fathoms deep,
  Where dead, forgotten things forever sleep,
And tumult of the waves comes never nigh,
And e'en beyond the glimpse of Day's great eye—
  To cling and clutch the ooze, thy task to keep
  My boat at rest, in front the self-same sweep
Of well-known coast, o'erhead the self-same sky.

Nay, rather, when the mighty winds are free,
  Be thou the needle, loyal to thy North,
    To bid my bark the utmost isles explore.
    Better go down amid the tempest's roar
  Than rot in land-locked bays, and put not forth
At hearing of the loud entreating sea.

TO DEATH.

I KNOW thou lurkest somewhere down the way,
  Specter, whom all men seek though all men dread;
  In some safe nook beside the path I tread
Thou sittest, grim, and day by weary day,
When shadows lengthen, "Surely," thou dost say,
  "He comes at eve;" at eve, unvisited,
  "To-night he comes;" and when the night is fled,
"And yet he comes, nor will he long delay."

Yea, Death, I come. But thou shalt not affright
  The forward fall of my unfaltering feet,
    Nor flutter the even coming of my breath.
  Not at the last as strangers shall we meet;
On hopeless ways, no helpful star in sight,
    I have already faced and proved thee, Death.

TO KANSAS.

NOT for thy outward charms of form and face,
  Careful to leave no feature unexpressed,
  As if for beauty's sake we loved thee best,
We bring thee praise; nor for thy pride of race,
Nor for thy wealth that waxeth great apace;
  Nor will we vaunt, with low and swinish zest,
  The milky richness of thy mother-breast,
Like unweaned babes that know no higher grace.

Shall we be lured by these things? Are not we
  A something more than mouth and eyes and ears,
    To eat and look and listen life away?
More than these skin-deep beauties must thou be,
  To win and keep our homage through the years;
    Yea, fair in more transcendent wise than they.

And fair thou art, as we would have thee be,
  Fair even in this more transcendent wise;
  The light of high communings on thee lies;
Thy touch the bond abide not, but are free,
Thy look is gracious, holy; none but thee,
  Smiled on howe'er she be by happy skies,
  Hath power to still the hunger of our eyes,
Unsated by the mountains and the sea.

For thou art Freedom's daughter, and thy birth
  Was through the pain of Righteousness's wars,
    Thy cradle song, the battle's roar and din.
Therefore thy beauty hath the greater worth
    Of noble thoughts; so art thou fair within,
  And claimest thine the pathway of the stars.

A. A. B. Cavaness.

MEMORIAL DAY.

Nature, sweet mother, loving all
With equal heart, forgetful twines
Her beauty round the battered walls,
And hides, with flowers, the battle lines.

In languid dream, o'er vale and hill
The daisies sentinel her dead;
Heedless for what they fought and fell,
Or by what banner they were led.

Her children were they all — dear boys —
For something good each heart beat true;
Brothers, yet at the bugle's voice
To battle marched in gray and blue.

Now in her arms the foes lie still;
  She grants them gracious covering:
With quarrel done, their sweet good will
  The happy birds forever sing.

O days of blood and jealous pain,
  You hurt our hearts full deep and long,
That still the bitter thoughts remain,
  Resentful of the costly wrong!

O noble heart, whose sacrifice
  Sealed gloriously the Nation's cause,
Whose thoughts, benevolent and wise,
  Are reverenced as the Nation's laws,

How have we imitated thee,
  Redeemed thy large and liberal word—
If malice banish charity,
  With hands still ready for the sword?

May incense of these roses fair
  That die in this sweet death of May,
With breath of balm load all the air,
  To heal the hearts of blue and gray.

'T is holy fragrance, fraught with fate
  Grander than dwells in steam and steel;
And builds the fabric of a State
  Worth all the woe that bought its weal.

So shall our heroes peaceful sleep
While love and honor, flowers and stars,
Through centuries their vigils keep,
Till love and honor banish wars.

SPRING.

UNDER the opened gates of Paradise
Now swings the world, and thro' the soundless seas
The wind-swept heaven drops upon the trees
The perfumes of celestial sacrifice;
O leaves and flowers — sweetest mysteries —
Thrilling our souls with voiceless madrigals,
Are ye not ciphers writ on Nature's walls,
The organ notes of future symphonies?

Prophet blossoms! Earth's winter has been long,
Eons of years, O emerald, preaching leaves,
Snow-banks of human hearts, glaciers of wrong!
But lo! it comes, the sun that all retrieves,
The ages' glass, the miracle of spring
Doth shadow Time's majestic blossoming.

LOVE.

THE challenge of the night's eternal bloom —
Planet and sun; this speck on which we crawl
In paths eccentric to our mystic doom —
Even as it, awhile in light, then gloom —
With dark arcana filled, whose subtle thrall
Doth bend us over rock and flower, and sweeps
Our wondering souls thro' universal deeps
Straining to catch their meaning mystical,
Are but as letters dimly streaming light
On Love — of all, the essence infinite —
The life of angels, and whose lack 's the curse
Of devils; but to mortals left to know
As both the bliss supreme and saddest woe,
Love is the secret of the universe.

POETRY is the struggle of the soul
Toward angels' speech — the soul-divining rod,
Invoking from all deeps their bliss and dole,
And shadows of the mysteries of God.

— *Cavaness.*

E. P. Chittenden.

SELECTIONS FROM "THE PLEROMA," A POEM OF THE CHRIST.

Book II, Christ in History.

THE PLEROMA.

Now hath our *Fullness*, immanent in time,
The promise of the first creation filled;
See nature upward turning to the sky,
To list the footsteps of its Creator!
Veiling our glories, and low bending down
We pass the open door into the earth.
Farewell, Eternal Father! We descend:
So hast thou willed, ere earth or man became;
Thou know'st the way, the sacrifice, the end.
Turn back, ye splendors of the heavenly throne!
The Son of God shall be the Son of Man;
The Timeless find and feel the bonds of time;
The Spaceless One shall tabernacle space;
The Increate be of a virgin born;
The Godhead bodily revealed to men.

ODE.

The Song of the Stars.

THE song of the stars,—the wondering stars!
The listening, glistening, diamond stars;
While the blithe, blue air
Calls everywhere;
To the hills and vales,
To the glades and dales:
"List, list, to the song of the wandering stars!"

The shout of the stars,—the numberless stars!
A glorified host with light-wingèd cars!
While the blithe, blue air
Calls everywhere;
Heralding far
The "Son of a Star!"—
The antiphone of the wondering stars!

The sigh of the stars,—the increate stars!
The wistful, mystical, soulful stars!
While the blithe, blue air
Calls everywhere,
"Behold Judea's STAR!—
Flashing his beams afar!
In his *trigon* of tears
A scepter he bears,
And the fadeless crown of the increate stars!"

Chorus of Angels.

He hath suddenly come to His temple;
  His hour and His mission's begun;
In the plenary graces of manhood,
  He shines like the orient sun.

Humanity, here is thy summit!
  Lo, here is the CROWN of mankind!
In this beautiful CIRCLE of virtues,
  Are SEVEN PERFECTIONS divined.

They seal Him the Son of the Highest!
  They sign Him the meekest of men!
They lend Him unspeakable beauty,
  That thrilleth and thrilleth again.

They praise Him the GOAL OF CREATION!
  The END of the timeless process;
The mystery hid from the ages —
  The SAVIOR a world shall confess.

His FAITH and His REV'RENCE perfect,
  Toward God; His OBEDIENCE too:
His LOVE for mankind most unselfish;
  His WISDOM, the Heavens shine through.

His HOPE, never dimm'd in the darkness;
  His VICTORY, full o'er Satan:
In sinless INCOMP'RABLE MANHOOD,
  BEHOLD HIM — THE PERFECT ADAM!

Gentle as a child — mighty as a God;
Peaceful as a fountain — wrathful as a flood;
Simple though His accents — deep as is the sea;
Loved by little children — dreaded MYSTERY!
Needy as a servant — richest born of beings;
Praying to the FATHER — almoner of kings;
Walking on the earth — dwelling in the sky;
Speaking in the fields — answered from on high;
Guide of all to life — leading unto death;
Promiser of Heaven — in His dying breath;
Friend of sinners, He — suffering their guilt;
Most divinely MAN when His blood was spilt;
Dying unto life — victor in defeat;
Raisèd from the grave to a heavenly seat.
Hail we! Hail we, Jesus! Mystery divine!
Thine the kingdom ever! And the GLORY Thine!

WHO HATH BELIEVED?

Or ever the angel's word
The fleet disciple heard;
Or ever the women cried:
"He is risen, the crucified;"
Or ever the eastern sun
Rose on Jerusalem;
In the empty sepulcher,
With the folded napkin there;
And the spicèd cerements
That gave forth their incense;

A voice within him spake:—
"Let the silent harp awake!
Let the eye of faith perceive!
Let the one He loved believe
In the risen Nazarene,
Though His form is yet unseen."

Then the Scripture poured its light;
And the dawn trod on the night;
And the effigies of grief
Were the voice that brought relief.

'T is a parable of love,
Which the humblest soul may prove.
Up, O heart! why dost thou grieve?
Though unseen thou canst believe;
And the Easter morning bring
Blessings from the risen King.

EUALGIA.

I WAS thoughtless till thou found me,
Always heedless till thou bound me,
Throwing loving arms around me,
Sweet, sweet pain.
I was mortal, but I thought not,
Rashly doing what I ought not,
Ever willing what I wrought not—
Sweet, sweet pain.

Visitor, heaven sent, I sue thee,
Tho' my racking members rue thee,
And my reason vain eschew thee—
Sweet, sweet pain;
Prythee, tell me ere thou leave me,—
For my sins weigh down and grieve me—
In thy arms will He receive me,
Sweet, sweet pain?

Peace! dear soul, the Savior hears thee,
In the passion ever nears thee,
On the changèd cross uprears He—
Sweet, sweet pain.
Heavenly Father, if Thou willest,
With my Lord, the cup Thou fillest,
I will quaff, until Thou stillest
Sweet, sweet pain.

—

BURDENS borne are soonest lightened;
Darkest skies are soonest brightened;
So the soul by faith is heightened;
Hope thou in God!

— *Chittenden.*

OUTWARD and inward; ebbing and flowing;
Phases are myriad; life is but one;
Circles concentric, meeting, and showing,
Higher than human, Nature hath none.

— *Chittenden.*

E. J. Crego.

FAITH.

'T WILL not be long.
The dewy morn will pass away
Before the scorching heat of day,
The flowers will droop, birds cease their song;
The sun will seek the golden west,
Behind the hills 't will sink to rest —
'T will not be long!

It is not far.
Beyond the clouds that veil the skies,
Beyond the mists that dim our eyes,
Faith sees a beauteous, gleaming star;
She hears the white-robed angel throng
Sweet strains of melody prolong —
No, 't is not far!

It is not wide,—
That current, death, that sweeps along,
So deep and dark, so swift and strong:
She hears the boatman cross its tide;
Safe, safe with Him, no more alone,
Oh! Joy supreme, sweet rest and home—
Aye, 't is not wide!

A COQUETTE.

Spring is sweet coquette:
With smiles and melting tenderness she comes
To storm, with bud and blossom, all your heart;
'T is useless to resist, or try escape.
The woodland fastness is her citadel,
Where every wingèd songster pleads her cause.
Nor yet shall you avoid her in the field:
For, kneeling at your feet, she 'll clasp your hand,
And, with the other, point to summer's golden prime,
And make rash promises of what the future holds.

Experience may tell you to beware—
To trust not her seductive promises,
To look not on her as she smiles or weeps;
Yet, ere you are aware, within your heart
She breaks the winter up,—and you are won.
Then, laughing at your weakness, she is gone
To try her countless arts in other climes.

Spring favors not deep thought; but, rather, sows
The seeds that ripen later into thought.
The soul seems nebulous, and scarcely feels
Its own existence in the universal joy;
But, basking in the sunlight, drinks deep draughts
Of this new wine of life
With which all nature seems intoxicate.

DESTINY.

MAN lacks resource;
The Great Designer never does.
Man cannot pierce the unexplored,
Beyond the confines of the universe,
To form creations of his own.
At best we only imitate God's works:
He ne'er repeats his own.
Are there two leaves alike in all the wood?
Two streams that run with equal murmur to the sea?
Two birds whose warblings are unvarying harmony?

We part to-day; God wills it so.
And though both journey o'er the hill,
Your path cannot be mine.
Our lives are like two ivy vines
That, clambering o'er the oak,

Cross and recross to gain the top.
Each point of intersection marks
The greeting of a friend,
A farewell spoken.

We part to-day. If we are friends
To-morrow we shall meet again,
And, clasping hands,
Take courage and press on,
The summit to attain.

Thomas Emmet Dewey.

THE ROSE'S MESSAGE.

I SAW her stroll alone in evening's shade,
And with a torn rose stem she slowly traced,
Upon a mossy wall, with lichens graced,
Some careful words. By her dear presence stayed,
I sought the meaning that the rose conveyed.
So stealing near, with footsteps lightly placed,
I held her close in loving arms embraced,
And read the message as she stood dismayed.
Ah! what a joyful tale it told to me,
Though tender eyes had hinted oft the same!
It filled my heart with rapturous ecstacy,
Thus dimly etched beneath my lowly name;
It was in very truth Fate's fond decree,
For rudely written there, I read, "Je t'aime."

HIS PLEADING—RONDEAU.

DEAR one, 't is sweet for me to trace
Upon thy tender, wistful face,
With glistening tears of sorrow wet,
But like a pearl with diamonds set,
A love that seems like Heaven's own grace.

And while I steal this fond embrace,
Within our old-time trysting place,
I know 't is wrong, so wrong, but yet,
Dear one, 't is sweet.

Oh! canst thou from thy mind efface
The wrong, and then with me retrace
The dear old way where first we met,
When life was free from vain regret,
And when the years flew on apace?
Dear one, 't is sweet.

HER ANSWER RONDEAU.

Yes, love, 't is sweet, as sweet to me
As it can ever be to thee,
Yet, lead me not too far astray—
Thine heart is wild, my will is clay,
But thou must wait till I am free.

'T is hard, this stern captivity,
This thralldom I couldst not foresee,
Oh! would that of it I could say,
"Yes, love, 't is sweet."

E'en though I yield in some degree,
I cannot grant thy loving plea;
So tempt me not, I meekly pray.
Perhaps, dear heart, somewhere, some day,
Before the world my song shall be:
"Yes, love, 't is sweet."

Ad. H. Gibson.

WHY WAIT?

WHY wait to show your love,
Until the form lies cold?
Why leave unsaid those words
Of dearer weight than gold?

Oh! could you read the heart,
And see love's hunger there,
You would not wait to speak
And show your tender care.

When death's chill brink is passed,
We'll heed not love expressed
By lilies cypress-twined
Across the pulseless breast.

PRAIRIE ASTERS.

STARRY blooms, your forms I greet,
Down where brook and prairie meet;
Purple, lilac, paler hues,
Gleaming thro' the Autumn dews.
Quails and doves come here to drink,
Where you love to nod and blink.

Prairie asters, fringed and bright,
Add to Autumn beauty-light;
Down the valleys, on the hills,
Fringing deep the prairie rills,
Asters bright, you bring sweet cheer,
Love to light the fading year.

TO EIGHTY-EIGHT AND EIGHTY-NINE.

WHAT hast thou left, Old Year?
A grave that holds one ever dear,
Where cherished dreams are laid away,—
December 's chilled my buds of May.
Thou left'st sere leaves and withered hopes,
A sombre vale where a shadow gropes;
A deed undone, a sad regret
That will not let my soul forget.

What hast thou brought, New Year?
Fair promise nipped by ghastly fear,—
Or will the flowers, that now seem dead,
On Easter morn lift up their head
And smile with resurrected life
Of joy, where deadly pain and strife
Had choked it out? I still will hope,
Though heart and soul 'mid shadows grope.

Lillie B. Gilliland.

ONE THING STANDETH.

YOUTH will quickly pass away;
Flowers bloom but for a day;
Brightest hopes will soon decay;
Life and earth death soon will sever,
But God's love, it faileth never.

Brightest hours too soon are gone;
Scarce they've come ere they are flown;
One thing standeth — one alone.
Though earth's best should pass forever,
God's rich love, it faileth never.

Thou who art forlorn, distressed,
Take this lesson to thy breast;
Hold it close; 't will give thee rest:
Naught of earth can from thee sever
God's rich love, it faileth never.

Allen D. Gray.

LIFE.

ONE time, when day's last lingering ray had faded,
  And murky clouds obscured each cheerful star,
And 'mong the distant hills by darkness shaded,
  I heard the whispering of the winds afar.

Upon the bridge that spanned a flowing river,
  I stood and gazed upon the outward flow;
I saw the shadows on its bosom quiver,
  Like phantoms rising from the depths below.

It tarried not a moment, downward sweeping,
  Out toward the bosom of the deep, broad sea,
Whose mighty billows 'gainst the shores were leaping,
  Tossing their foaming spray perpetually.

—

Life is a current setting toward the ocean
  Of the Unknown: that sea without a shore;
Where all the tumult of this world's commotion,
  Is hushed to stillness in the evermore.

And curious Science, through the passing ages,
  Vainly hath sought the mystery to unfold;
But not to earth's philosophers or sages
  Have been the secrets of that voyage told.

For He alone, whose wisdom guides our being,
  Who placed within its transient home the soul,
When from its clayey tabernacle fleeing,
  Will 'cross that trackless waste its way control.

OLD DAYS AT SCHOOL.

OLD days at school! What scenes arise,
  Recalled anew from Youth's fair morning,
Radiant and fresh to Memory's eyes,
  And beautified by Hope's adorning—
    Old days at school.

Old days at school! When life was fair,
  And Fortune offed all her guerdon;
Ere dreams had flown, or brooding Care
  And Sorrow had imposed their burden—
    Old days at school.

Old days at school! With eager feet
  We wandered 'mid the groves Illyrian,
Where Knowledge, in her far retreat,
  Should yield to us the cup Pierian—
    Old days at school.

We're older now, and life has grown
A trifle frayed about the edges;
"Alas!" we sigh, "I might have known
That Time would not redeem his pledges
He made at school!"

Indeed, perhaps it may be true,
For Fortune *is* a fickle rover.
If so, her flight we will not rue,
Nor mourn the days we can't live over—
Old days at school.

And after all we may not sigh,
For Faith is real and duties nearer,
And we shall find that, by and by,
Even Heaven itself may be the dearer
For days at school.

THE VOICE OF THE TIME.

I.

No sound of war's alarms,
No strife of hostile arms
Vex'd the deep hush of the historic morn,
When He—erstwhile foretold
By prophet bards of old—
The Wonderful, the Prince of Peace, was born.

II.

Now wakes th' triumphant song
Of the angelic throng,
Now shines the natal star with bright'ning ray;
The radiant morning waits
Beyond her crystal gates,
To give the world its primal Christmas day.

III.

From out the ancient night
Springs the prophetic light,
The dawning of the Golden Age appears;
The wrathful voice is still
On Ebal's cloudy hill,
The curse is lifted from the dolorous years.

IV.

Perpetual glory fills
The spaces of the hills,
The paths the humble Galilean trod,
The healing hand to reach,
Love's benison to teach,
Man's sovereign hope, the fatherhood of God.

V.

With charity and cheer,
The swift recurrent year
Its gracious Christmas message shall repeat,
Till peace and Christ's good will
Th' regenerate earth shall fill,
And Love's eternal purpose is complete.

Mary Tenney Gray.

COUNTRY CHILDREN.

ONLY a tangle of nut-brown hair,
A maze of arms uplift and bare,
A scamper of feet, all swift and brown;
Thus they differ from those in town.

Now after the calves, now high in air,
A-flitting here and flying there,
Lading the wind with maddest glee,
As full of fun as full can be.

Up in the loft where the swallows hush,
Out where wintergreen berries blush,
High on the hill where ripe berries glow,
Deep in the swamp where blue flags grow.

Falling asleep on a cock of hay,
Risking necks or running away;
Hunting what next they can do or dare,
Full of frolic and free as air.

We grieve for the loss of youth so fair,
As every country child may share—
Whenever we walk the city street
And watch the tread of children's feet,

So poised and posed by a master's art,
Threading their way through hall and mart.
Daintiest ruffle and silken gown
Are not so fair as free arms brown.

Satin and kid on pallid, slow feet
Are far less fair than brown ones fleet;
And tiniest hands in "Jouvin's best,"
Daintily clasped in affected rest,

Are not so fair as plump ones free,
Clasping fruits or swinging from tree.
Country mothers, by the brown sun-bloom
Save their darlings from early tomb.

No city man or woman can see
Country children, wild with their glee,
Without a sigh for the rugged steep
Where mosses hang and roses creep;

For craggy ledges where sweet ferns grow,
And paths are white with arbutus-snow;
A sighing thought for that walk in the dew,
Through earliest clover fields he knew;

A yearning wish for the old refrains,
The long-hushed songs, and long-lost games;
A waft of new-mown hay at the door—
The soft sweet-brier's breath once more;

The rare perfume of the cinnamon-rose,
The breath of all the garden grows;
The twitter of swallows, cooing of doves,
And alas! perhaps, a sigh for dead loves!

DEAD LEAVES.

Drift the dead leaves gaily by,
Falling low or circling high:
Brilliant maple red as blood,
Tawny gold of cottonwood,
Softest bronze of poplar leaf,
Deepest browns of grass and sheaf.

Youth and verdure both have fled—
Glory, color—Death instead
Making merriest holiday!
Just as each will pass away—
Wildest carnival ere Lent—
Robed like reveler, Death is sent!

Out of Youth's bright land will burst
Tender leaves of life at first;
Later, cometh fruit and bloom,
Richest hue and best perfume:
Scarlets hot, from Passion lent,
Azures soft, from deep Content,

Yellows gay, from Envy's star,
Royal purples, won in war,
Darkest sacramental wine
Spilled betwixt the thorn and vine;
Every leaf like missal rare
Gilt or dyed by grief or care.

Once we paint the life leaves o'er,
Sybil-like we ope the door;
Scatter wide and fling them high,
Richest woof and rarest dye.
Brightest gold will surely show
Breath of furnace heat below.

Who will count the life we bring
To color deep the wreath we fling?
Who shall know the depths of woe
Tingeing all the leaves we throw?
Who will care that thorns we pressed
Gave that rosy leaf its best?

Only so the deeds we do
Help a comrade safely through;
Let the leaves so bright and dead,
Tell of all the life we led
'Mid the joy of Autumn hour
When fruit was shed, and closed the flower.

Let the leaves, so dyed and dead,
Bravely sink to their last bed —
Gorgeous, like some king of old,
Cased in cinnabar and gold;
While our life-leaves softly fall,
With dear Love above them all.

LOVE IS DEAD.

"PAN is dead!" the cry went ringing,
  And through groves of cypress fell,
Hushing all the Grecian singing
  And planting rows of asphodel.

Love is dead! yet birds are singing,
  Love is dead! yet flowers bloom;
And the sunlight, summer bringing,
  Cannot light his darkened tomb.

Love is dead! He died in anguish,
  Of a sharp and cruel blow,
And, howe'er your heart may languish,
  Love shall warm it never, no!

No eye saw the stroke 't was given,
  No ear heard the mortal groan,
When the tender heart was riven,
  Bleeding, desolate, alone.

No lip read the funeral service,
  No bell tolled the final sigh;
Mass or anthem ne'er above us,
  God and Grief alone watch'd by.

And you might have had him living,
  Warm and close, to clasp and hold.
Life's sole gift, that's worth the giving,
  By your words, lies dead and cold!

Charles Moreau Harger.

ATLANTIS.

PROUD isle of the long distant ages,
  Weird land of philosophers' dreams,
Thy name, in all history's pages,
  With mystical radiance gleams;
Enchantment her glamour of glory
  Has cast like a mantle o'er thee,
As Time hath repeated thy story,
  Lost Gem of the Sea,
            Atlantis,
  Atlantis! Lost Gem of the Sea.

Bright sunshine no more gilds thy mountains;
  Thy slopes are enshrouded in night;
Undiscerned are thy clear, gushing fountains,
  Once crownèd with seven-hued light;
All hushed are thy bird-notes, once gladly
  Resounding o'er valley and lea;
Slow tides through thy forests sweep sadly,
  Lost Gem of the Sea,
            Atlantis,
  Atlantis! Lost Gem of the Sea.

Sunk in ruins, thy palaces nestle
  Where finny tribes fearlessly roam;
Far above thy rich fields the staunch vessel
  Sails swift through the high-tossing foam:
Thy monuments, fallen and shattered,
  Can give to tradition no key;
The threads of thy banners are scattered,
  Lost Gem of the Sea,
        Atlantis,
  Atlantis! Lost Gem of the Sea.

Thy sons lie at rest 'neath the waters,
  Their tombs 'mid the coral groves placed;
And with them repose the fair daughters
  Whose presence thy mansion-halls graced.
All at peace are thy foes and defenders;
  Side by side sleep the slave and the free;
What now are thy kingdoms or splendors,
  Lost Gem of the Sea?
        Atlantis,
  Atlantis! Lost Gem of the Sea.

What scenes of earth's newness elysian
  Were rimmed by the curve of thy shore,
Ere came mighty Nature's decision,
  "Stand thou before heaven no more?"
What tales of heroic endeavor,
  What wisdom of won'drous degree,

Are sealed in thy bosom forever,
Lost Gem of the Sea?
Atlantis,
Atlantis! Lost Gem of the Sea.

Great mother of nations unnumbered,
Once teeming with manifold life,
For centuries past thou hast slumbered,
Unmoved by the surge's hoarse strife.
Man's curious questionings scorning,
Close-hidden thy secrets shall be,
Till thou greetest eternity's morning,
Lost Gem of the Sea,
Atlantis,
Atlantis! Lost Gem of the Sea.

THE SOD SCHOOL HOUSE.

An earthen mound on the prairie's swell,
The work of rough settlers' hands,
An uncouth temple for learning made,
Its walls of the rudest earth-squares laid—
A lone sod school house stands.

Not a tree in sight from the open door,
Not a shrub on the landscape's face,
But a sea of grass fills all the view,
Its waves are of emerald's sparkling hue,
And above cloud-shadows race.

I hear the sound of a tinkling bell:
 'T is the teacher's signal sweet,
There 's a drowsy hum from a score of lips,
There 's a smothered laugh at some dullard's slips,
 And a noise of restless feet.

Do they think as they tread the earthen floor,
 Those children gathered there,
How near to Nature's true heart they stand,
Their tan-stained cheeks by her light breath fanned,
 Their eyes on her features fair?

Do they hear the notes forever new,
 That the limitless prairies sing?
'T is a nobler strain than books have told,
Than choirs have breathed or organs rolled,
 Or silver chimes can ring.

They say: "Be pure as our morning dew,
 Be firm as our leagues of earth,
Be kind as our breezes that gently blow,
Be bright as our hills in the sunset's glow,
 Be gay as our song birds' mirth.

"Look up to the light like the spears that wave
 O'er all our stretching miles;
Let the flowers that dimple our bosom cast
A spell of beauty that shall at last
 Tinge manhood's years with smiles."

And the peaceful haze at yonder rim,
  Just kissing the prairie sea,
Has a soft refrain for the song of life —
It whispers, "Beyond this earthly strife
  Lies the glorious rest to be."

Can the youthful ears but catch the hymn,
  Can the hearts its lesson glean,
With what wealth of soul to the world they 'll go
From that earth-walled school room, cramped and low,
  'Mid the hills of lustrous green.

A SONNET.

YON peaks that Titan-like so high uplift
  Their lordly heads above the rain and mist,
  Seen by a rich supernal splendor kissed;
Some solar gold seems o'er their sides to sift,
As glimpse we catch through lazy cloudlet's rift;
  But those whose paths do summitward insist
  Bring naught from all the slopes that there exist
But clay — dead clay, like that of lowland's drift.

So fortune's favored sons have to our eyes
  Some seeming tinge of glory half divine,
Yet Time, all-undeceiving guide, denies
  That they but with a borrowed luster shine —
The dust in which their souls so proudly reign
Is counterpart of ours that walks the plain.

Lillie H. Kellam.

CARDINAL NEWMAN.

THROUGH dusky arches floats thy pleading hymn,
Till all the air
Grows tremulous for light o'er pathways dim;
The waves of prayer,
Led by the glory of the Eternal Day,
Break at thy feet which late have found the way.

Thrice happy thou beyond these boundaries
Of doubt and sin,
Whose adamantine crags forbidding rise
O'er fens within,
Where many a peril waits the unwary soul,
So slowly faring toward the heavenly goal.

For thee the angels' smile, the cloudless day,
The harps of gold,
Before whose strains earth's shadows flee away;
Ere back hath rolled
The tide of prayer to these dull shores of night,
Strew thou thereon some gleams of kindly light.

Hattie Horner.

THE GREAT DELIVERANCE.

Calm Egypt slept. The veil of heavy night
Hung darkly 'tween the desert and the sky.
Above the sleeping land that dreamed no harm,
The sullen clouds bent low and threateningly,
And through the darkness and the silence deep
No voice of solemn warning breathed aloud:
"Prepare to meet thy God." The soft night wind,
That crept from house to house with noiseless tread,
Repeated not: "Thy first-born all must die."
The bird that moved upon the midnight bough
Said not: "The hour is come"—nor yet the stars
That stood above the land. The night wore on,
And Egypt slept.

The night wore slowly on,
And Israel, by the dimly burning light,
Did watch with anxious heart. The lamb was slain
And on the lintel had the blood been struck;
The cloth was spread; the hurried meal was passed.

With girded loins and ready-sandaled feet,
The eager bondsmen waited, longed and hoped—
They knew not what.
And now the hour was come.
The murky veil of night was torn by wings
Of God's destroying angel swooping down
To smite the land—and Egypt slept no more.
A sudden cry broke on the air. 'T was not
The anguish of a single stricken heart:
It rang from house to house, and swelling rose,
A mournful chorus, a funereal wail,—
The voice of Egypt mourning her first-born.
The angel passed. Death hovered in his wake,
But Israel's blood-stained door was left uncrossed.
Night wore away. The stars above the land
Went dimly out; and lo! the rising sun,
Whose latest dying ray had looked on slaves,
Saw Israel out of bondage—free at last.

Years, ages have rolled by. A deeper night
Enfolds the land in darkness and in gloom.
Above a careless world that dreams no harm,
The clouds of sin stoop low and threateningly
And Justice whets her keen avenging aword.
Still Egypt sleeps. God's awful warning words,
"The day thou eat'st thereof thou'lt surely die,"
Forgotten are. The scornful idler laughs,
Unheedful that the hour is drawing nigh.
O men! O brothers! are you faithful, true?

Your candles, are they burning? Do you watch
With girded loins, with anxious, hopeful hearts?
The Lamb is slain; and if His saving blood
Be on your lives, the angel will pass by,
And with the rising sun you'll quit
Your bondage for the precious Promised Land.

KANSAS: 1874—1884.

(Written upon the departure of the corn train from El Dorado, for the relief of the Ohio flood sufferers, April 6th, 1884.)

1874—PER ASPERA.

CHEERLESS prairie stretching southward,
Barren prairie stretching north;
Not a green herb, fresh and sturdy,
From the hard earth springing forth;
Every tree bereft of foliage,
Every shrub devoid of life,
And the two great ills seemed blighting
All things in their wasting strife.

As the human heart, in anguish,
Sinks beneath the stroke of fate,
So at last, despairing, weary,
Bowed the great heart of our State;
She had seen her corn blades wither
'Neath the hot wind's scorching breath;
She had seen the wheat heads bending
To the sting of cruel death.

She had seen the plague descending
 Through the darkened, stifling air,
And she bent her head in sorrow,
 Breathing forth a fervent prayer;
And the fierce winds, growing fiercer,
 Kissed to brown her forehead fair,
While the sun shone down unpitying
 On the brownness of her hair.

Then she looked into the future,
 Saw the winter, ruthless, bold,
Bringing her disheartened people
 Only hunger, want and cold;
Looking, saw her barefoot children
 Walk where snow sprites shrink to tread;
Listening, heard their child lips utter
 Childish prayers for daily bread.

Low she bowed her head, still thinking
 O'er her people's woes and weal,
And the ones anear her only
 Heard the words of her appeal;
Send that faint cry onward, outward,
 Swift as wire wings can bear:
"Sisters, help me, or I perish—
 Heaven pity my despair!"

HATTIE HORNER.

1884—AD ASTRA.

Verdant wheat fields stretching southward,
Fruitful orchards east and west;
Not a spot in all the prairie
That the springtime has not blessed;
Every field a smiling promise,
Every home an Eden fair,
And the angels—Peace and Plenty—
Strewing blessings everywhere.

As the heart of Nature quivers
At the touch of springtime fair,
So along the State's wide being
Thrilled the answer to her prayer.
She has seen her dauntless people
Ten times turn and sow the soil;
She has seen the same earth answer
Ten times to their faithful toil.

She has felt the ripe fruit falling
In her lap from bended limbs;
She has heard her happy children
Shouting their thanksgiving hymns;
She has seen ten golden harvests;
Now, with grateful joy complete,
She has poured the tenth, a guerdon,
At her benefactors' feet.

Thou can'st not forget, O Kansas,
All thine own despair and woe;
Who hath long and keenly suffered
Can the tenderest pity show;
Not in vain the needy calleth —
Charity her own repays,
And "thy bread, cast on the waters,
Will return ere many days."

Peace, thine angel, pointeth upward,
Where the gray clouds break away;
And athwart the azure heavens
Shineth forth Hope's placid ray;
Look to heaven and to the future —
Grieve no longer o'er the past;
Through thy trials, God bless thee, Kansas,
See, the *stars appear at last!*

SELECTIONS FROM "ILA."

And on and on she read till it was done, —
This tale of sacrifice and inward strife,
And anguish deep and self-forgetting love, —
Till "Passed the strong, heroic soul away."
Then, with a sigh, she laid the volume down
And there was silence. Nina broke it first.
"If Annie had been true to him," she said,
"A little longer, — but a year or more, —
The story might have ended well. Oh, why

Will faith decay when hearts have but to wait?"
"The sorest trial that Love is called to bear
Is waiting, hopeless waiting," Cecil said,
"And Rutherford perhaps was right, if Hope
So well sustains the heart of him who waits.
For otherwise, throughout the waiting time,
Must Love feed on itself and wear away."
Then spoke Rasalle:

"Fie on the changeful heart,
That touched by Love and bound by Honor's ties,
Cannot be true an half score years or more.
And what though Hope should set? I know a flower
That, nodding to the westward-sloping sun,
With steadfast purpose turns before the dawn
To greet his entrance through the eastern gates.
And what though Love should ebb? Does not the shell
That 's flung upon the dry and senseless sand
Forever keep the wooing of the sea
Within its heart? I know a Book that says:
'Pay that which thou hast vowed; 't is better far
Thou shouldst not vow, than vow and pay it not.'
And we were right, for it is Constancy
That best sustains the heart of him who waits."

"But what is this you sanction?" Nina cried,
"A hopeless waiting,—Honor stripped of Love,
The payment of—it might be—light made vows,
Mere steadfastness of purpose,—nothing more.
Perchance some strange perplexities would rise,

And even sorrow and misfortune dire,
To haunt the keeping of some thoughtless vow.
For human destinies have countless threads,
And each life has its pattern planned of God.
How can we know if through our neighbor's web
Are woven threads of our own weal or woe?
And who can stop his busy Weaver's hand
To find if all the woof be his or not?
And who so rash to break or tie one thread?"

"Vows are not lightly made in Honor's realm,"
Rasalle made quick reply, "The Mount of Life
Is steep and high, and many faint midway.
Sweet manna falls in plenty at its foot;
Hope's dews are bount'ous; Joy breathes on the air.
Here bide the dwellers of the valley land,
Content to grope their narrow twilight way,
To live, to die. Here dwell th' inconstant hearts,
The restless murm'ring people who cry out:
'Up, make us gods!'—who worship but by sight.
Ah! Love itself can live but half the way,
Upon the breathless heights great souls must climb,
If they would reach the goal. Yea, there's a point
Where friendships, human sympathies, and all
Save Duty's self must fall at last below
The snow line of that rare and lofty realm.
But oh! the trumpet of the Voice divine,
From out the thund'rings of the awful cloud,
Speaks only to the fasting soul that stands
On Honor's Sinai, serene, alone!"

J. Lee Knight.

SELECTIONS FROM "RESURGAM," A DECORATION DAY POEM.

Earth unto earth!
Such is and has been since the dawn of time,
The sum of knowledge and the end of life.

Dust unto dust!
No power is potent to bear down the wall—
No mortal vision e'er hath pierced the gloom,
Or passed the portal to what lies beyond.

Ashes to ashes!
The cycle ended, once again the earth
Takes up her burden to renew the round.

And is this all? Must earth forever claim,
With mandate changeless, all there is of life?

The grave, in closing o'er the body dead,
Shut out forever from both sight and sense
The form and being of what once was man?
Is there not something left of life—some thought
Or aspiration which survives the tomb;
Some hope or purpose—some undying love,
To span the chasm between life and death?

*   *   *   *   *   *

What do we honor by these solemn rites?
The dust and ashes of the earthly forms,
Dissolved and scattered at the touch of death?
Can these see beauty in the bloom of flowers?
Are these attuned to harmony of song?
Or hear they words of sacred, holy prayer?
Our homage rather, with its song and praise,
Like incense rising from an altar fire,
Ascending upwards from the lifeless clay,
Seeks out its object in the vital spark
Which glows with radiance of immortal light—
The MAN that liveth when the body dies!
The glorious purpose that inspired the life—
The aspirations toward the good and true—
The deeds of valor—and the acts of love—
The priceless offerings at freedom's shrine!
These we may honor—these be deathless things—
Ourselves we honor, while we honor them.

Earth unto earth!
And yet it is not all—there still remains,
Surviving matter in its changing forms,

That inspiration which defies the worm!
A fadeless amaranth that blooms for aye
In wreath immortal round the martyr's brow!

Dust unto dust!
But still like sunlight through the rifted clouds,
Above the grave a golden halo gleams,
Which lights us onward like a beacon star
To higher, holier, purer thoughts of life!

Ashes to ashes!
But still, like fountain from the smitten rock,
Or crystal waters from a hidden spring,
There comes a current from the dews of death
Which gently laves the fevered brow of care,
Which stills the throbbing of the pulse of strife
And turns the thought, in restful sense of peace,
To contemplation of the Great Unknown,
The sum of wisdom—and the Source of All!

APOTHEOSIS HISTORIÆ.—THE UNSEEN REALMS.

A CHRISTMAS POEM.

"THERE 's a magical realm where the sun goes down,
Behind the blue sea in the west;
Give me ships to sail in the name of your crown,
Give me warrant to claim your majesty's own,
And I will go forth to the quest!"

So plead the Genoese — the brave — the ideal,
The Argonaut, hopeful and grand;
And the queen made reply to that daring appeal —
"I pledge my own jewels, the crown of Castile;
Go! find me that beautiful land!"

The warrant was signed, and the mariner brave,
With a willing, yet doubting band,
Sailed afar in his ships o'er the pathless wave,
Sailed onward and westward, till e'en he misgave
Of finding the mystical land.

On the altars of hope the fires burn low —
The sun still goes down in the sea;
Yet courage, brave hearts! ye are not to foreknow
What the magical realm hath in store to bestow;
Its glories ye may not foresee.

Press ye forward in faith, for the morning light
Yet may gild with its golden sheen
The beautiful land that lies hidden from sight,
And fruition of hope may your patience requite,
In that magical realm unseen.

At last, from aloft, comes the glad cry of cheer,
"Land in sight," and the weary one,
Who erst radiant with hope, or trembling with fear,
Had so patiently sailed o'er the pathless mere,
The goal of his hope had won.

"There's a beautiful realm that ye have not seen,
There's a city with streets of gold;
There are valleys that bloom in perpetual green,
There are harvests full ripe for the reapers to glean,
In that land ye are yet to behold.

"In that realm there is rest for the weary hands,
For the toilers whose work is done;
On the shores of its rivers gleam golden sands,
On its mountains a temple eternal stands,
Whose altar fires burn as the sun.

"In that radiant land shall the blind eyes see,
By the light of an endless day,
And the nations be healed, the bond be made free,
And the fountains of life, as the tides of the sea,
Shall flow on forever and aye."

So spake the old prophets of Israel's race,
The sages, the wise and the true—
And their message of hope to new light gave a place
In life's darkness, as stars in the darkness of space,
Give their light from beyond the blue.

"We will seek this new realm by land and by sea,
By fire and by sword, night and day;
Our flocks and our herds at your service shall be;
Before us the tribes and the nations shall flee—
Go! lead us, we know not the way!"

So answered the legions, yet sought they in vain,
They found not the Kingdom of Light:
Their ships sailed afar o'er both river and main—
They marched over mountains, through valley and
No tidings came out of the night!

Dread pestilence, famine, and red-visaged war,
As age after age they press on—
Till lo! from aloft, through the portals ajar,
Gleams out o'er the darkness the Bethlehem Star,
To tell of the coming of dawn!

— —

As that mystical realm beyond the blue sea
Was seen in the vision of old,
So that realm unseen, in the time yet to be,
Beyond the dark river, in visions we see,
In that city with streets of gold!

We are voyagers who sail o'er a stormy main;
We are seekers for realms unseen;
As the sower who soweth shall reap again,
Either harvest of thistles, or golden grain,
So, also, our harvest we glean!

SELECTIONS FROM "TWO PICTURES: A CENTENNIAL POEM."

WEDDED to Freedom on her hundredth birthday!
  Mature in years, and life aglow with health,
Bright buds of hope are blooming on her pathway
  Prophetic promise of her future wealth!
Her home—a continent of God's creating.
  Her dower—primeval Nature's boundless store
Of soil productive, and rich mines awaiting
  To lay their buried treasures at her door.
Her pride—the mem'ry of the noble martyrs,
  Whose blood baptized the realm of liberty.
Her strength—a serried host of sons and daughters,
  Whose hearts and arms are nerved by loyalty.
Her glory—freedom of the humblest person
  Who breathes unfettered from the taint of crime.
Her power—the written law, blest Freedom's charter,
  That guards her people's rights in every clime.
Her shrine—the sanctuary of myriad hearth-stones
  Whence prayer or praise ascends. Her faith—the creed
That God vouchsafes to every soul created,
  Such free oblation as it choose or need.
Her wealth—the wisdom of an age supernal.
  Her hope—the genius of the good and true.
Her flag—a symbol of the stars eternal,
  That deck the vaulted dome of heaven's blue!

Her trust—the keeping of the truth immortal
 That Right and Justice, with their chastening rod,
Are guardian angels of the waiting portal
 That opens upward to the throne of God!
Our Mother! be thy future destiny
To wield the scepter of a world made free!

Philip Krohn.

INVOCATION TO SLEEP.

Night's dull silences are throbbing from the mountain to the sea,
Thou hast lulled a world's wild tumult, yet thou comest not to me.

Lightly on my evening pillow, whitely on my tired hand,
Creeps a wandering wave of moonrise, ere it burnish all the land.

From the purple-hooded midnight star eyes languish into mine,
With the dew of tender memories dripping all their downward shine.

Till the tempted life within me swoon, beneath the sensuous rain—
Swoon a moment, ere it flutter back to wakeful hours again.

And my soul, impaled, and panting 'mong the captors, pleads with thee,
That thine arms uplift and bear me safely 'cross the thought-ridged sea;

Through the gates of the unreal, on whose rare and radiant
shore,
Flash unnumbered shapes of beauty, fair as Eden ever wore.

And our lost loves walk and wander, by the waters cool and
clear,
Till forgotten how the passions sweep their sorrow tempests
here.

Come to me, invisible charmer! from the shadows come
to me!
Night's dull silences are throbbing from the mountain to the
sea.

Flower and leaf nod tremulously to the wind's low lullaby;
Bird and bee their wings have folded—sweetly restful all
but I.

Summer woods have ceased their waltzing—hushed and
slumbrous all the land;
Only elfins dance and dally o'er the moon-bedizzened sand.

Through the dim and dewy midnight, coy enchanter, steal to
me—
Steal from out thy mystic hiding, whether cloud or wave
it be;

Whether weird and witching moonbeam, or the vapor on
the hill,
In thy chaste embrace enfold me, that my spirit roam at will.

Where but blooms immortal brighter o'er some rare and radiant shore,
And, from lute of unseen minstrel, music quiver evermore;

And our loved and lost ones linger by the waters cool and clear,
Till forgotten all the bondage that enslaves life's purpose here.

A YEAR'S REVIEW.

Failure and only failure,
  Each step of the crooked way,
And the wrecks — I dare not count them —
  On the shore of every day.

Though the mist seemed shaped as goblins,
  In the moon's uncanny light,
As I glance with a touch of heart ache,
  O'er the backward paths to-night,

Failure and only failure,
  Over and over again —
With my high resolves dismembered,
  And lost on the reckless main.

And the words I should have spoken,
  And the deeds I should have done,
Confront me at every gateway,
  In the new paths just begun.

I have said that my fields should blossom —
  The fields I had thickly sown
With seeds of a noble promise;
  But a wind, from some cloud outblown,

Breathed over them and they withered,
  And my soul cried out with pain!
For it was all failures, failures,
  Over and over again.

In the yesterdays that vanished
  Ere yet I could call them mine,
They were gilded cups full brimming
  With white, rare-flavored wine.

They had dripped from joy's pure vintage,
  As the gales of hope swung by;
But others the nectar tasted,
  With a smiling lip—not I.

Shall the new tides dashing onward,
  'Gainst the rocks where dashed the old,
Yet toss on the shore of gladness,
  For my reaching hands to hold?

Or shall a bolder grasp it,
  And my own be empty still?
Gray tides on the cold sands breaking,
  For your sweet wines I am ill.

If I knew there were shoals in waiting
  To grapple the careless keel
Of my bark o'er the young year's currents,
  Till with wounds it writhe and reel,

As a dove by an arrow stricken,
I should shrink from each waiting morn;
For more than the scent of roses,
The sting of the rose tree's thorn.

AUTUMN.

Now the shadows lengthen early,
And the birds that with us stay,
Ill at ease and anxious seeming,
Sing not as they do in May;
For the winds suggest the keenness
Of the winter days so nigh,
And the trees stand bare and lonely
As the leaves drop off and die.

Now the squirrels are most busy,
Whisking here and leaping there;
Gleam their colors in the sunlight,
Sounds their chatter on the air;
And with busy feet and restless
Lay they up their winter store,
'Gainst the time when snow will cover
Sheltered wood and open moor.

Now the denseness of the forest
Lessens as the days speed by,
And, in search of game, the sportsman
Listens to the quail's lone cry.

And church steeples in the distance,
  And towns lying far away,
And blue lakes, gleam before us,
  That lay hid for many a day.

Ah! when summer's day is ended,
  And the strength of spring is spent,
And the frame of man, so sturdy,
  'Neath the weight of time is bent,
May not man pass like the autumn,
  Fading out in colors rare,
And from heights of contemplation,
  See a future large and fair.

Mrs. E. S. Eaton Loomis.

OUR HOLIDAY.

WE 'RE very "tired, my heart and I."
So long we 've toiled, and all in vain,
We fear;—but just beyond our pain
We see, beneath a brighter sky,
Our holiday.

Shelter, and rest, and all good cheer,
Are there. Ah me, 't is hard to wait!
Hasten, O Death, and ope the gate,
So we may have, in that high sphere,
Our holiday.

VIA CRUCIS.

WITHOUT, life's shadows darkly fall,
Gloomy, and gray, and chill;
Within, the air is all aglow;
Within, my spirit's ill
Is healed by Holy Will;
Without, I ne'er could find a balm
To heal the wounds it bears.

And yet I know that prayer and praise
Are not the whole of life;
The soul must gird its armor on
And go amidst the strife
With fiery dangers rife—
Must fight its way to heaven's gate,
A soldier of the cross.

A BATTLE WELL LOST.

A theory may be abandoned; a conviction must be fought for.—*Beckwith.*

"The soldier of truth never surrenders; his ship's colors are nailed to the mast."

In cloudless skies the May-day sun shone fair,
The while with steadfast, peaceful look he said:
"Is there not room among the holy dead
For him who does his best? A few must dare,
And vanquished fall, and thus the way prepare;
Then, hosts to Truth's slow victory are led;"
And forth with most unselfish hopes he sped,
With earnest faiths, and with ideals rare.

In clouded skies the wintry sun shone dim,
The while I watched a single ship outbrave
A hostile fleet. . . . The ship went down at last,
With cannon's roar in place of burial hymn,
With all her colors flying at the mast,
And he who nailed them there, beneath the wave.

Frank A. Marshall.

A MOTHERLESS GIRL.

OH, why cannot mothers look down from above,
And shelter and shield with their infinite love
The orphaned and desolate left on the earth,
Too lately esteeming and knowing their worth?
If Heaven e'er weeps at a sight that is sad,
A sight that would render its gladness less glad,
'T is when, in the roar of the world's busy whirl,
It weeps at the sight of a motherless girl!

No love of a father, tho' tender and warm,
Can shelter and shield from the world's beating storm.
What touch is so tender, what voice is so dear —
The touch and the tones of the one we revere?
What hand can smooth for us the pillow of care,
And pluck from our pathway the thorns that grow there?
God pity and guide, in the world's busy whirl,
That orphan of orphans — a motherless girl!

Ah! priceless and placeless that mother that left
Alone and defenseless that daughter bereft!
In hours of affliction, in seasons of care,
When burdens grow heavy — too heavy to bear,
Oh, where, in that season of sorrow, can go
The heart that is tempted to yield to its woe?
Save God's, there's no strength 'mid the world's busy whirl
To shield and to shelter a motherless girl!

Though far she may stray from the ways of her youth,
From Purity's path, from sweet Virtue and Truth,
Though sin may take from her the flower of her fame,
And plant in its place the hot blister of shame,
Yet God, in his mercy, writes after her name,
In the book of her guilt and the record of blame,
Till the Judgment the tear-blotted record unfurl,
This token of pardon: "A MOTHERLESS GIRL."

MARBLE AND SAND.

AN act of wrong had steeled my wounded heart,
Whose trusting faith had been betrayed
By him on whom that trusting faith was staid;
And fierce resentment ruled the better part
That cried, "Forgive!" With firm, relentless hand,
That drew its angry strength from trampled pride,
I reared a high, enduring stone, to stand
Throughout the passing years; and on its side

I blazoned all the tale of trust betrayed.
But all the waters of repentant tears,
And beating surge of all-effacing years,
Could not erase the record I had made.
And when my burning anger cooled to gentle blame,
That chiseled record fanned it into flame!

A gentle deed, that should have blessed my lot,
And taught me to forgive and made me kind,
Was scarce remembered in my anger blind,
But ere it had been done was straight forgot.
For, burning with the hate of outraged pride,
I wrote the deed with careless, heedless hand,
Not where the lasting stone the years defied,
But in the changing, ever-shifting sand.
And when the billows of the passing years
O'er both the written records swept and rolled,
The gentle tale, that would have then consoled,
Was washed away with my repentant tears.
The deed I would forget was still in lasting stone;
The deed that I would still remember,—gone!

Ah, so it is! In hard, enduring stone
We grave our wrongs with anger-guided hands;
While gentle deeds are written on the sands,
To be forgotten ere those deeds are done.
On both the stories fall repentant tears;
But one remains, to mock our keen regret,
Unsoftened by the wearing fall of years;
And one is gone that we would not forget!

Ah! better far we grave the actions kind
  In granite lines, with eager, grateful hand,
  And write our wrongs upon the fickle sand;
And when we read the written archives, find
The tale of Love triumphant o'er the surge of years;
The tale of Hate effaced by gentle tears!

SWEETER AND DEARER.

Oh! dear to our hearts are the friends that adore us,
    Whom tender affection esteems;
But dearer, the friends that have journeyed before us
    To the shore that we tread in our dreams.

Oh! sweet are the warm and affectionate presses
    That strengthen the hearts that they thrill;
But sweeter, the touch of the spirit caresses
    From the lips that are silent and still.

Oh! warm is the clasp of the thrilling affection
    Of hands that we hold in our own;
But dearer by far is the sweet recollection
    Of the clasp of the hand that is gone!

How prized are the warm, loving glances we cherish,
    From eyes that are beaming to-day;
But ne'er from our hearts can the memory perish
    Of the smile that has vanished away.

Though footsteps of loved ones may thrill us with pleasure,
And gladden the hearts that are sore,
Our spirits more fondly the memory treasure
Of the step that shall thrill us no more.

Though sweet are the tones of the tender affection
That cheer the sad spirits they thrill,
Yet sweet through our souls rings the dear recollection
Of the tones of the voice that is still.

Though fragrant the perfume of flowers we have gathered
From gardens of pleasure or love,
Oh! sweeter the fragrance of flowers that have withered
But to bloom in the gardens above.

Oh! tender the song that the birdling is singing
Of melody filling the air;
But sweeter, the music through memory ringing
Of a joy that has changed to despair!

Joel Moody.

JOHN BROWN.

SAD Linn! Dark plots and direful things
In secret hatched, and compacts made
In the vile den or sickly shade,
And writ with point of Slavery's blade,
In bloody book which Treason brings.

In this black book appears the name
And sentence of each Freedom's son—
Boldly in blood the letters run,
In the fierce hand of Hamilton.
Now stands to his infernal fame

The record of that bloody book.
Eleven blasts from hell are blown—
Eleven teeth of dragon sown—
Eleven sons like grass cut down;
And Hydra of his feast partook.

Then came John Brown close on his path,
  And boldly passing to his den
  Him struck an awful blow, and when
  The shackles broke and fell from men
He writhed and roared in demon's wrath.

Eleven slaves are now set free—
  A kindly stroke for those who fell—
  A just and righteous parallel—
  Their freedom won, and strange to tell,
Kansas has gained her liberty.

Not on far Afric's burning sand,
  When age on age has come and gone,
  And people searching in the throng
  Which passing centuries prolong,
Ask for some hero proud and grand,

The theme for master sculptor's hand
  Whose ancient glory and renown
  The waiting multitude shall crown,
  Will there remote appear John Brown;
But will be found in every land

His glory heralded by seers—
  In marble cut; by poet sung;
  And his rude image shall be hung
  Round the charmed neck, and every tongue
Shall praise him as the saint of years.

And here, in Kansas, we shall raise
  The statue of undying fame.
  With sculptured art, we shall proclaim
  The fond memorial of his name,
Which thus shall stand and speak his praise.

The man—the sword—the Hydra slain—
  The hand outstretched to greet
  The needy one—the face replete
  With love—and, underneath his feet,
The broken links of Slavery's chain.

Bright star of Kansas! Now thy place
  Is fixed: a brilliant central gem,
  In Columbia's diadem;
  Which, like the star of Bethlehem,
Points out a savior of the race.

O Slavery! dire, enraged; if you
  Are doomed, what serves to now rebel?
  What serves the powers that wait on hell?
  You sent the shaft when Sumpter fell,
Which, on recoil, shall pierce you through.

—*From "The Song of Kansas."*

THE PATRIOT'S LOVE.

Proud Kansas! known on land and sea;
  Happy the man on foreign strand
  Who hails from thee! In any land
  On earth, a Kansan let him stand;
This name shall be his passport free.

Kansas! I love thy sacred name,
  As o'er my memory sweeps the past;
  From thy dark, deep trouble thou hast
  Now come to glorious peace, and vast
Domain, and everlasting fame.

I dearly love thy stately frame;
  That grand physique of prairies wide,
  Which, like some undulating tide
  Of mighty sea, billows in pride
Thy lovely form, and breathes thy name.

I love thy soul—that spark divine,
  Which, struck from the Almighty Mind,
  Illumines earth with manners kind,
  And motives pure, and laws refined,
And justice sure, and love benign.

The home of freemen thou shalt be,
  Where patriot footsteps love to stray,
  And to thy soil their homage pay,
  Where Virtue, with her heavenly ray,
Doth shine in sweetest purity.

And, when Time comes to end my days,
  Chant in my ear some old refrain
  Of patriot song; the parting pain
  Will cease; then say: "In humble strain
He sang for Kansas her sweet praise."

—*From "The Song of Kansas."*

THE TEAR.

She, weeping, dropped a tear, and when it fell
  A poet caught the little pearly sphere
  And questioned it; and his enraptured ear
Caught up the things which it began to tell.
He heard the tone of solemn sounding knell
  O'er a departed hope; the cry of fear;
  The wail of anguish, and soft sighings dear,
Which make the lover's lonely bosom swell.
And there he saw, ensphered, a mother's heart,
  Bleeding for her lost child; and open grave,
And love amid the trophies of his dart,
  With every throb of passion that it gave.
All heights of joy, and depths of woe, were here
Encompassed in the ocean of a tear.

YET sweet it is for us to know
That flowers do live beneath the snow;
And Winter always hath its Spring,
When flowers will bloom and birds will sing;
And souls we love will grow more fair,
When silver threads come in the hair.

—*Moody.*

BUT what is great and what endures
Is built by all.

—*Moody.*

Ellen Patton.

GRAPES OF ESCHOL.

At the borders of the Promised Land,
Where Jordan spreads her shining sand,
They camped along the river side
And saw beyond the river's tide
The grapes of Eschol hanging fair;
But even then they did not dare
  To enter in and boldly eat.

They sent the spies across to bring
The purple globes that climb and cling
Upon Judea's sunny hills,
And all their musky fragrance spills
As incense on the sun-steeped air;
They longed to taste, but did not dare
  To cross the Jordan with their feet.

Not faith enough to keep the track,
And so the dear Lord turned them back;
Eschol's sweet grapes they could not win,
Because they feared to enter in.

How oft we stand and look across
To Paradise, and count the cost,
  And to the desert turn again.

And yet how often we might eat
The fruits of "Beulah Land," so sweet;
The spies bring back the clusters rare,
They gather in our nights of prayer;
Come, let us linger on the shore,
Until we cross the river o'er
  And lose each earthly stain.

Oh, Eschol's grapes, I press thy wine,
Till all these border lands of mine
Grow sweeter, fairer as I drink;
My feet but linger on the brink
Of Jordan's bank; I soon will go
Beyond the river's narrow flow,
  To heaven's emerald plain.

A LUMP OF CLAY.

ONLY a little lump of clay.
And it lies in the potter's hand;
He looks at it, he looks at the wheel,
With its burnished edge of sharpened steel,
Knows how the cruel touch will burn,
Yet will hold it down and turn and turn;

Then turn and turn with a loving touch—
The clay will break if ground too much.

A well-shaped vase, made from the clay,
Again 't is poised on the master's hand;
"Good wheel, I praise thee for thy share,
But little vase, there is more to bear.
Thrust into the flames that brightly glow—
A mighty breath on the fires doth blow,—
Dost think me a master hard and stern,
As I thrust you in to burn and burn?"

Would you know it now for the lump of clay
That lately lay on the potter's hand?
The flames grew cool and he drew it out,
Lovingly then he turned it about.
The fire had given an added grace,
You knew by the smile on the master's face;
What if the vase had not held still
While the cruel fires did all their will?

Once but a lump of moistened clay
That the potter could toss from his hand;
Now it is touched with the royal dyes
That mock earth's bloom and mirage the skies;
You might almost think the bird would soar
Out from the vase and up from the door;
A monarch's hall it is fit to grace,
Since it felt the wheel, and the fire's embrace.

Man is only a lump of clay,
Till the Master Potter takes him in hand;
To-morrow will come, to-day will go,
The bud of the rose begins to blow.
Then, wheel of my fate, you may turn and turn,
And fires of love, you may burn and burn;
Some must command, and some must obey —
God is the potter, and I am the clay.

THE PRIEST AND SATAN.

THE incense was burned out, but the fragrance lingered still;
The organ ceased its throbbing, yet held the music's thrill;
One single taper burning, and the shadows gathered fast,
While worshipers went slowly out; the services were past.

The mystic cross gleamed whitely and caught the taper's shine,
While stainèd glass of window panes shone out like ruby wine;
Even the murky shadows had caught a radiant glow,
But the Devil lurked in corners for Angelo's overthrow.

A slender, dark-haired priest alone was kneeling now,
The heavy sweat of agony was beading on his brow;
The whitened lips half opened seemed whispering in prayer;
A Devil in the corners, but Christ was in the air.

Did grief gnaw at his vitals, or the shadow of some sin?
Like a sleuth hound swiftly follow a soul to lose or win?
All night before the sculptured Christ he lay in silent pain,
Until the shadows fled away and morning dawned again.

Then pent-up thought found utterance in cries and anguished
words,
That mingled with the fleeting of morning's singing birds:
"Jesus, who in the wilderness wast tempted without sin,
My strength is gone; vigil and fast the victory will not win.

"I love a woman, that my woe; O Christ of woman born,
Come in and help me keep my vow upon this sacred morn;
But is it sin? I cannot tell, but this one thing I know,
That, having vowed myself to Thee, I cannot let Thee go.

"Thou art my Bride, O Princely One, and in Thy starry eyes
I catch the rays of love divine; my hell is paradise.
How did it come about? you ask. Thou knowest that full
well;
She comes to my confessional, her whitened sins to tell.

"The fairest thing God ever made; a glory in her hair,
And on her brow the raptured look that only saints should
wear.
I chanted holy hymns to Thee till vaulted arches rang;
She listened then as if she thought the white-robed angels
sang.

"I charmed her heart away, O God, and she drew out my
own;
I dare not yield it up to her, it 's anchored to Thy throne;
My vestments touched her in the aisle; it stung me with a
thrill;
That shows how weak a mortal is, how puny human will.

"The Devil whispered, 'You can fly, and with that voice
could win
Plaudits from men and yellow gold;' *he* says, 'it is not sin.'
Ah, scaly Devil, dost thou think that thou canst win me so?
I 'll hurl the Bible at thy head: go, grinning horror, go."

The matin bell begins to ring, the shadows glide away,
One penitent comes down the aisle in gown of silver gray;
She kneels before the latticed guard: "My Father, I con-
fess—"
A sudden pause to clasp white hands across her throbbing
breast.

"What is it, daughter, let me hear?" The priest bent low
his brow,
Caught the flash of diamond ring and knew the suppliant
now.
"I have not breath to name my sin; absolve and let me go;
I love a tall and stately priest; his life is pure as snow."

Swift silence stung the lang'rous air; Satan stepped softly in
With sensuous eyes and smirking mouth—another chance
to win;
For even church walls will not keep this subtle vagrant out;
Only the Christ, once crucified, can put this fiend to rout.

Angelo parleyed with his foe; alas, was almost won;
Before him lay a crucifix with image of God's Son;
He gazed at it and sprang erect; his hands were clenched with pain;
His pale, set lips were stained with blood; he hissed, "What, back again!"

A shape unseen by other eyes stood plainly out for him;
The Devil tried a saintly smile; it turned to demŏn's grin.
The suppliant waited, but the priest dropped by his chair to pray;
When he uprose his hair so dark was turned to ashen gray.

He kissed the crucifix and spoke: "In peace, my daughter, go;
Baptised in Jesus' crimson blood, your sins seem white as snow."
The rustle of her silken gown died out upon the air;
The priest had conquered, but the man lay fainting in his chair.

"And did he die?" I hear you ask. Ah, no, the verger came,
With holy water bathed his brow, the breath came back again;
The aureole of whitened hair forevermore would be
A signal from the heights of pain — a badge of victory.

He saw his Eve and was unmoved; she looked at him with awe;
The people talked among themselves and wondered what he saw
That bleached his hair in one short night, and touched his human face
With such a holy, raptured look — almost a saint-like grace.

Yes, men go down and fight with hell, but rise to glory's height;
When Christ stoops down and touches them, Satan is put to flight.
Angelo's conflict is a type. If it should come to me,
I could not conquer in the fight, unless God set me free.

AND since those days, how many hearts have bled,
How many souls climed up the heights of time?
Pain carving out the steps from earth to God:
For all He loves must pass beneath the rod.

— *Patton.*

Thomas Brower Peacock.

THE GARDEN OF THE MIND.

Oh, weed the weeds unsightly
  From the garden of the mind,
That flowers of thought bloom brightly
  In beauty fair enshrined.

That the fragrance of those flowers
  Waft in glory o'er the earth,
And forever through the hours
  Lead to better, brighter birth.

That the angels all immortal,
  In their purity and grace
Smile adown from heaven's portal
  On the wondrous human race.

"IT IS I, BE NOT AFRAID!"

God's beauty, grand, supernal,
Far in the starry depths unfurls!
God's glory lives eternal
Above the crash of mighty worlds!
Wafts o'er the grave's abysmal shade:
"It is I, be not afraid!"

O Conqueror of Death! O Light!
The stars that seem to speak in ruth,
Unto Thy radiance are but night—
But froth and foam on sea of truth!
Christ calls to all—to Peter said:
"It is I, be not afraid!"

The night passed on—the fourth watch came—
Christ glorious walked the troubled wave;
They saw Him coming like a flame,
And cried for fear a ghost to brave;
"Be of good cheer!" their dear Lord said;
"It is I, be not afraid!"

I hear the courser's thundering tread!
The shouting of the armèd foe!
I saw the vanquished as they fled
In their sad misery and woe—

But hark! a voice their sorrows stayed:
"It is I, be not afraid!"

Though ships are tossing on the sea,
Though winds are running wild and high,
Though fishermen on Galilee
Are fearful when the storm is nigh—
O deep His meaning! more than said:
"It is I, be not afraid!"

MAN.

The history of the human race
Is but a tragedy of tears!
Man's life 's a passing breath, I trace,
Where always jostle hopes and fears.

As barque tossed by the stormy sea,
High on the foam-capped wave is hung,
One moment more, and lost 't will be,
Engulfed for aye—by all unsung!

So man each hour stands on death's brink,
Unto himself a mystery!
An instant stands, then down doth sink,
Lost in oblivion's somber sea.

Then boast not of thy power, O man!
  Thou art no more — no more shall be
Compared to God, the Mighty, than
  A second to eternity.

God secretes in places lone and still
The rarest products of His will;
For contact with the world disarms
His fairest flowers of half their charms.

— *Peacock.*

Noble L. Prentis.

IN LIFE'S AFTERNOON.

'T WAS IN life's afternoon
  I loved thee, dear:
The hopes of morn had fled
  With midday clear.
Illusion's veil was rent,
Dreams fled too soon,
When came the sweet event,
And in life's afternoon
  I loved thee, dear.

Gone was the morning dew,
  The mists that hid.
Life's frowning peaks
  Rose dark and near:
The sun the springs had dried,
The sands were hot and drear,
When, in life's afternoon,
  I loved thee, dear.

Soon had night's shadows come
 With shapes of fear;
Soon had the darkness fallen,
 But ere
Day's curtain downward rolled,
The sky flashed rose and gold,
And, in life's afternoon,
 I loved thee, dear.

William Haskell Simpson.

BABY MARIQUITA.

Hush-a-bye! hush-a-bye!
Bees have left the fragrant rye,
Clouds are fading in the sky;
Home the weary birdies fly —
Hush, baby dear,
Soldiers rest from war's alarms,
All is quiet on the farms —
God's peace clasps us in its arms.
Sleep, mother 's near!

Hush-a-bye! hush-a-bye!
Moonlit silence wraps yon hills,
And this river feels no thrills
From the still wheels of the mills —
Hush, baby dear.
You, too, find soft-billowed rest
On sweet mother-love's warm breast,
When rose flushes quit the west.
Sleep, do not fear!

Hush-a-bye! hush-a-bye!
Quickly pales this harvest moon,
Life is all a jangled tune,
Wake not from youth's dreams too soon--
Hush, baby dear.
Toil may hurt you, by and by;
Joy bring heart break; laugh bring sigh—
Love bends low to soothe each cry.
Sleep, I am here!

TRIUMPHS.

In youth's new years of sowing time,
All breezes blew with swing and rhyme;
And onward, upward was the climb.

What seas beyond those mountains lay:
What triumphs, and crown wreaths of bay,
Were mine, if dawned another day!

Ah me! Unnumbered days have passed,
And still uncrowned, unknown, at last
I journey down the hillside fast.

Snug in a home, my very own,
A wife to make lone hours less lone,
A little child, bone of my bone.

This is the quiet end of all
The old-time strife and hurting fall —
Love holds me in its pleasing thrall.

Yet not the close! My precious boy,
In unrestrained and childish joy,
Is playing with some curious toy:

For him my old ambition burns,
For him my heart in silence yearns,
As one by one life's ways he learns.

He, too, in part these paths will tread:
May he press on, sure-stepped, ahead,
To where the victor's cheeks blush red!

LOVE RENEWED.

So MUCH to do ere hands are cold;
So far to fare, ere limbs grow old;
So much to say, if all is told —

That we lose sight of better things;
Forget, in earthward wanderings,
To use love's buoyant sweeping wings.

And I — yes, I sometimes forget
To lure away your care and fret,
And kiss the cheeks by teardrops wet.

Here let us pledge ourselves anew,
Each to the other, open, true,—
Lest life lose all its rainbowed dew:

Who knows what time we say good bye?
When one shall in the churchyard lie?
A star gone out of joy's bright sky.

Florence L. Snow.

ACCEPTANCE.

As THE spirit of the seed,
Be it germ of flower or weed,
Palm or willow, oak or pine,
Yellow grain or clinging vine,
Waits within its bit of earth
For its rightful hour of birth,
Drawing strength from day and night,
Reaching upward into sight,
Living in a sweet content
With its whole environment,
Destined nothing else to know
But in its own place to grow—
So the soul of man should be,
Accepting thus his destiny.

As the essence of the clod,
Molded by the hand of God,

Be it part of hill or plain,
Lying in the sun and rain,
Cherishes a royal rose
Or a wondrous fruitage shows,
Blending by its alchemy
Elements of mystery,
Knowing nothing but to yield
To the purpose half revealed,
And to use its mystic power
Higher functions to endower—
So the soul of man should be,
Accepting thus his destiny.

As the marvel of the light
Shining from the Infinite,
Be it sun or be it star,
Held within its golden bar,
Fills its own allotted space
With a miracle of grace,
Giving inspiration breath
Through the silences of death,
Guiding in each measured course
Currents of creative force,
Knowing but divinity
In its work of ministry—
So the soul of man should be,
Accepting thus his destiny.

CREATIVE POWER.

WITH A BUNCH OF POND LILIES.

I SEND these lilies, poet, unto thee,
All dewy-fresh from cool Nequempo's breast,
Where they were anchored tenderly at rest
By rootlets far below where I could see
The prison birth that left the blossoms free
To draw from mold and slime, at God's behest,
The beauty that in all things He has blest.
O miracle of love, that this should be!

Such is the wonder of creative power,
That lies, O friend, within thy being's core,
And brings from life's dark ooze the perfect flower
Of poetry, which sheds its royal store
Upon the wide world's bosom, to endower
Poor human kind in ways unknown before.

KANSAS.

FOR A PICTURE.

A GRACIOUS figure, clad in living green,
Enwrought with gold, and broidered thick with flowers!
A woman, strong in woman's noblest powers,
Who holds the scepter of a fearless queen,

And there is love in her blue eyes, I ween—
  The love that keeps a watch from its own towers,
  And on her lips the purpose that endowers
Her royal children with her royal sheen!

Above her floats a gonfalon, unfurled,
  That men may see her colors from afar,
And read therein her message to the world;
  Steadfast she stands, be it in peace or war,
Nor falters not though heavy clouds be hurled
  Athwart the glory of her guiding star.

Eugene F. Ware.

THE WASHERWOMAN'S SONG.

In a very humble cot,
In a rather quiet spot,
In the suds and in the soap,
Worked a woman full of hope;
Working, singing, all alone,
In a sort of undertone,
"With a Savior for a friend,
He will keep me to the end."

Sometimes happening along,
I had heard the semi-song,
And I often used to smile,
More in sympathy than guile;
But I never said a word
In regard to what I heard,
As she sang about her Friend
Who would keep her to the end.

Not in sorrow nor in glee
Working all day long was she,
As her children, three or four,
Played around her on the floor;

But in monotones the song
She was humming all day long,
"With the Savior for a friend,
He will keep me to the end."

It's a song I do not sing,
For I scarce believe a thing
Of the stories that are told
Of the miracles of old;
But I know that her belief
Is the anodyne of grief,
And will always be a friend
That will keep her to the end.

Just a trifle lonesome she,
Just as poor as poor could be,
But her spirits always rose,
Like the bubbles in the clothes,
And though widowed and alone,
Cheered her with the monotone,
Of a Savior and a friend
Who would keep her to the end.

I have seen her rub and scrub,
On the washboard in the tub,
While the baby sopped in suds,
Rolled and tumbled in the duds;
Or was paddling in the pools,
With old scissors stuck in spools;
She still humming of her Friend
Who would keep her to the end.

Human hopes and human creeds
Have their root in human needs;
And I would not wish to strip
From that washerwoman's lip
Any song that she can sing,
Any hope that songs can bring;
For the woman has a Friend
Who will keep her to the end.

QUIVERA KANSAS,

1542–1882.

In that half-forgotten era,
With the avarice of old,
Seeking cities that were told
To be paved with solid gold
In the kingdom of Quivera—

Came the restless Coronado
To the open Kansas plain
With his knights from sunny Spain;
In an effort, that, tho' vain,
Thrilled with boldness and bravado.

League by league, in aimless marching,
Knowing scarcely where or why,
Crossed they uplands drear and dry,
That an unprotected sky
Had for centuries been parching.

But their expectations, eager,
Found, instead of fruitful lands,
Shallow streams and shifting sands,
Where the buffalo in bands
Roamed o'er deserts dry and meager.

Back to scenes more trite, more tragic,
Marched the knights with armor'd steeds;
Not for them the quiet deeds;
Not for them to sow the seeds
From which empires grow like magic.

Never land so hunger stricken
Could a Latin race remold;
They could conquer heat or cold —
Die for glory or for gold —
But not make a desert quicken.

Thus Quivera was forsaken;
And the world forgot the place,
Until centuries apace
Came the blue-eyed Saxon race,
And it bade the desert waken.

And it bade the climate vary;
And awaiting no reply
From the elements on high,
It with plows besieged the sky,
Vexed the heavens with the prairie.

Then the vitreous sky relented,
  And the unacquainted rain
  Fell upon the thirsty plain,
  Whence had gone the knights of Spain,
Disappointed, discontented.

Sturdy are the Saxon faces,
  As they move along in line;
  Bright the rolling cutters shine,
  Charging up the State's incline
As an army storms a glacis.

Into loam the sand is melted,
  And the bluegrass takes the loam,
  Round about the prairie home;
  And the locomotives roam
Over landscapes iron belted.

Cities grow where stunted birches
  Hugged the shallow water line,
  And the deepening rivers twine
  Past the factory and mine,
Orchard slopes and schools and churches.

Deeper grows the soil and truer,
  More and more the prairie teems
  With a fruitage as of dreams;
  Clearer, deeper, flow the streams,
Blander grows the sky, and bluer.

We have made the State of Kansas,
And to-day she stands complete—
First in freedom, first in wheat;
And her future years will meet
Ripened hopes and richer stanzas.

JOHN BROWN.

STATES are not great except as men may make them.
Men are not great except they do and dare.
But States, like men, have destinies that take them—
That bear them on, not knowing why or where.

The WHY repels the philosophic searcher—
The WHY and WHERE all questionings defy,
Until we find, far back in youthful nurture,
Prophetic facts that constitute the WHY.

All merit comes in daring the unequal,
All glory comes from daring to begin.
Fame loves the State that, reckless of the sequel,
Fights long and well, though it may lose or win.

Than in our State, no illustration apter
Is seen or found of faith and hope and will.
Take up her story: every leaf and chapter
Contains a record that conveys a thrill.

And there is one whose faith, whose fight, whose failing,
Fame yet shall placard on the walls of time.
He dared begin—despite the unavailing,
He dared begin, when failure was a crime.

When over Africa some future cycle
Shall sweep the lake-gemmed uplands with its surge;
When as with trumpet of Archangel Michael
Culture shall bid a colored race emerge;

When busy cities there, in constellations,
Shall gleam with spires and palaces and domes —
With marts wherein is heard the noise of nations —
With summer groves surrounding stately homes —

There future orators to cultured freemen
Shall tell of valor, and recount with praise
Stories of Kansas and of Lacedæmon,
Cradles of freedom, then of ancient days.

From boulevards o'erlooking both Nyanzas,
The statued bronze shall glitter in the sun,
With rugged lettering:

"JOHN BROWN, OF KANSAS:
HE DARED BEGIN;
HE LOST — BUT, LOSING, WON."

SELECTIONS FROM "NEUTRALIA."

There is something in a flag, and a little burnished eagle,
That is more than emblematic, it is glorious, it 's regal.
You may never live to feel it; you may never be in danger;
You may never visit foreign lands and play the *role* of stranger;

You may never in the army check the march of an invader,
You may never on the ocean cheer the swarthy cannonader;
But if these should happen to you, then, when age is on you pressing,
And your great, big, booby boy comes to ask your final blessing,
You will tell him: Son of mine, be your station proud or frugal,
When your country calls her children, and you hear the blare of bugle,
Don't you stop to think of Kansas or the quota of your county,
Don't you go to asking questions, don't you stop for pay or bounty,
But you volunteer at once; and you go where orders take you,
And obey them to the letter, if they make you or they break you;
Hunt that flag and then stay with it, be you wealthy or plebeian;
Let the women sing the dirges, scrape the lint and chant the pæan.
Though the magazines and journals teem with anti-war persuasion,
And the stay-at-homes and cowards gladly take the like occasion,
Don't you ever dream of asking, "Is the war a right or wrong one?"
You are in it, and your duty is to make the fight a strong one,
And you stay till it is over, be the war a short or long one.
Make amends when war is over, then the power with you is lying;
Then, if wrong, do ample justice—but that flag, you keep it flying.

If that flag goes down to ruin, time will then, without a warning,
Turn the dial back to midnight, and the world must wait till morning.

* * *

I can give you a prescription that will always make a hero:
Go and get a full-fledged lover and reduce his hopes to zero;
Get a man that loves a woman with devotion pure and steady,
Let the woman "go back on him," and your hero is all ready.
Now just turn him loose and watch him: see old Cerberus, he cringes!
See! the red-hot gates are beaten from their solid brazen hinges,
And hell's blue platinum standards he is sabering into fringes.

* * *

All communities are cannon — intellect is ammunition;
Man is simply a projectile, flung with more or less precision,
And the more you jam him down, if he only has the powder,
Why, the higher up he goes and the gun it roars the louder.
And the globe sight of that cannon is a woman, and her station
Is to give the rash projectile proper flight and elevation —
To the sky or to the mud it must go at her dictation.

* * *

Any man is brave with money; braver far is he without it
Who dares always act uprightly, and not fret himself about it.
We should keep our faith and courage; if calamities assail us,
If misfortunes swoop down on us, like the vultures of Stymphalus,

It will never do to weaken, it is cowardice to fly them;
Do like old Troilian Ajax—strike an attitude, defy them.
If we waver and fall back, Fate will ever then be urging
Us like quarry slaves at nightfall, homeward to our dungeon
scourging.

THE anchors are strong that hold the ships;
The wire is strong that bridges the fall;
But all of their strength must suffer eclipse
Compared with the words of a woman's lips,
For she binds the man that has made them all.

— *Ware.*

WE all believe in Kansas; she 's our State,
With all the elements to make her great—
Young men, high hopes, proud dreams—'tis ours to see
The State succeed to what the State should be.

— *Ware.*

Will. A. White.

SENCE IDY 'S GONE.

SENCE Idy's gone somehow you see
The hours is longer 'n they usto be,
An' days an' skies are duller, an' the night
Drips out in oozing seconds drearily
At every hollow clock tick, till the light
Laps up the murky fancies wearily,
And fever'd dreams 'at come long after dawn
Mix up the happiness I hoped to see
'Ith that great sorrow which is hantin' me:
'At Idy 's gone.

Sence Idy's gone I dist can't stay
In doors; it seems like ev'ry way
I look I find some doin's 'at 'uz her'n:
Her apern mebbe, er the last croshay
She done before she went; at eve'y turn
I run acrost her mem'ry, so 's I say
I keep out doors dist kindo 's if I 's drawn,
An' hang around the crick here ev'ry day;
But even it keeps singin' in its play
'At Idy 's gone.

Go into town er to the store,
It's all the same, I hyur the roar
The crick is makin' as it reshes past
The bend; I know its sayin' somepin' more
'N folks believe, an' more 'n most folks dast,
'Less they believe 'at spirits crosses o'er
An' talks 'ith us; the housework do n't git on
Keeps gittin' tangleder 'n 't was before,
Dist like my head 'at 's tangled to the core,
Sence Idy 's gone.

A TWELFTH MONTH IDYL.

EVERY thing a-freezin' up, 'long about December;
Willer Crick amongst the rest, 'f I do n't disremember,
Froze up tighter 'n a brick, 'ceptin' where Bill Oldum
Throwed a whoppin' rock er stick, 't' see if it 'ud hold him;'
Slick ez glass an' green an' thick, temptin' an' a-teasin';
Hear it poppin' up the crick while it 's still a-freezin';
Hear the clinkin' of the skates, comin' thro' the timber—
Nosey Jim an' Shorty Bates 'll soon be gittin' limber.
I kin say now I 've begun, "'f I do n't disremember,
Willer Crick's the place fer fun, 'long about December."

Build a big ol' driftwood fire, sizzlin' an' a-smokin',
Fer the girls to stand around, shiv 'rin' an' a-chokin',
Till their fellers prances in, with some quirl erruther,
Sayin': "Shan't we try agin; go a little futher,

Up the slew er round the ben', 'way from where the crowd is,"
Er some sich like words — an' then — well, you know jes' how
't is —
Fer you orto see the ice, Satterdays an' sich days:
Looks jes' like a nest of mice, runnin' ev'ry which ways.
Ar debatin' club looks sick, fer 'bout ev'ry member
Sneaks off down to Willer Crick, 'long about December.

Afternoons when school is out, 'bout a hundred fellers,
Rat'lin skates an' dinner pails, headed by Jack Sellers,
Comes a-pilin' down the bank, an' before you know it
Give their straps a twistin' yank, an' away they go it —
Some a-cuttin' curlycues, some a-playin' shinny,
Some a-runnin' like the duce after little Skinny
Johnson, who 's a being "it" in some game erruther;
Cross tag, mebbe — I fergit — can't tell which from tuther;
But they 're having fun, you bet, more 'n in September,
Fur they do n't get overhet, 'long about December.

Then the fellers with their girls, haint they more 'n happy —
Girls 'ith cheeks an' lips so red, and 'ith eyes so snappy —
Skatin' up an' skatin' down, dodgin' folks 'at pass you;
Skatin' where they's no un 'roun', no un to harass you.
Willer Crick boys wa 'nt' much good, 't raisin' Ned and larkin',
But you bet they usta could beat the world a-sparkin'.
They 's a piece I heard tell of, says 'at young men's fancies
Lightly turns to thoughts o' love, in the spring; the chances
Are the reason this was sed, is 'at we remember
In the spring the fun we 've hed 'long about December.

THE OL' WOOD PUMP.

THEY 's differ'nt things about a farm 'at takes a feller's eye;
Some think 'at pigs is pickchuresk, though durned if I see why;
An' others thinks 'at bleating sheep an' wabbly-leggèd colts
Is proper things fer folk to paint; but that jest somehow jolts
On my artistic feelin's, bein' raised, y' understand,
On "Rock of Ages," "Plate of Fruit," an' "Views from Holy Land."
But speakin' of yer music, now I guess you hav' to hump,
If you beat the laffin' gurgle of
the ol'
wood
pump.

It used to stand behind the house right near the ellum tree,
Though summers 't was n't shaded much it did n't seem to me,
Fer afternoons it was so hot it jest 'ud burn yer feet—
I mean the platform 'ud; an' then you never saw the beat
Of how it lickt the wotter up before you 'd pumped a spell,
An' my! but wa 'n't the wotter cool from way down in the well;
You most could taste the coolness, an' yer taster 'd give a jump
To meet the wotter bubblin' in
the ol'
wood
pump.

The han's 'ud wash there mornin's, an' the stock 'ud come at night,
To drink ez fast ez Lige could pump an' work 'ith all his might.
The cattle they 'd injoy it, though, an' when they 'd got enuff
They 'd stick their noses in the troft an' pull 'em out an' snuff.
So when the stock 'ud go away, an' Lige was perty hot
He 'd stop the spout a runnin' 'ith his hand, ez like ez not;
He 'd pump a bit, then shet his eyes, an' put his mouth down plump,
An' drink a stream of gladness from
the ol'
wood
pump.

An' when you had to prime it, then they was an awful fuss;
The girls 'ud git the wotter pails and make a dredful muss,
Spillin' more outside 'n in; you could hyur it splashin' down,
Dashin' round aginst milk things 'ith a holler, far off soun';
Perty quick the pump 'ud snifle; then he 'd sorter turn an' growl;
Then, ez if he did n't like it, he 'ud jes' git up an' howl;
An' before you hardly know'd it 'ud hyur a little thump,
An the wotter 'ud be flowin' from
the ol'
wood
pump.

My stock of heroes never wuz
So very big, you see, becuz
I never understood the plan
'At they are built on; an' a man
Don't like to keep things 'round 'at he
Can't 'preciate — at least that 's me.

— *White.*

Kansas Symposium.

CRADLE OF FREEDOM.

MEN said—a noble few—that Kansas soil
Should yield its fruitage but to freeman's toil;
And Freedom, cradled here, grown great and strong,
Rose in her might to cope with ancient Wrong.
"Set free! Set free!" she cried, nor stayed her hand
Till only Crime wore chains in all the land.

—*Ellen P. Allerton.*

KANSAS, most loved of Fortune's guests,
Child of our hopes and fears—
Kansas, whose genius ever wrests
Victory from Failure's tears—
Thy children hail thee as the best,
And will for ceaseless years.

—*J. W. D. Anderson.*

A SIX line rhyme on Kansas, did you say?
One cannot sing her glories in a day.
Nay, more! let all the authors of our State combine
They could but mention Kansas in a six-line rhyme.

—*H. W. Bailey.*

As Venus walks the evening sky,
Fair queen o'er many a sister star,
O'er glows at morn, while shadows fly,
Bright herald of Apollo's care:
So shines our Kansas—though radiant stars her sisters are,
She reigns for aye, a nation's vesper and auroral star!

—*Mary L. Bard.*

A Norway legend tells us how, when the earth was done,
God called His angels to him; and lo! it chanced that one
Perceived one spot unfinished, and back to heaven went,
And, to his Master's service, the best of heaven sent.
So as the first is after, the last shall come before;
Kansas got that blessing: what could she covet more?

—*Lillie Binkley.*

THE LAND OF MEN.

Broad plains of Kansas, yoeman's pride, by battle stained,
'T was here that outraged Freedom rose, when bondage waned.
Thy sacred soil, O patriot land, is leader's ground,
Where Moral Right her proud head rears, no longer bound;
As first for Freedom, first for right, Godward we ken:
Demanding courage, hero's ground, thou makest men!

—*Carl Brann.*

The State, to Freedom sworn, that set the floods in motion,
Whose shoreless billows soon the Nation overran,
And washed away the lie, fulfilled the fine devotion,
Writ in our fathers' vow of loyalty to man.

—*A. A. B. Cavaness.*

KANSAS, ON SOME FUTURE DAY.

Come, mark me what I say!
Kansas, on some future day,
Will stand in the lead of all
Municipalities on this ball,
Both in art and agricultural line,
For hers is a destiny sublime.

—John Preston Campbell.

I sit upon a summer cloud. My car
Unseen I float, and view the lands afar,
To choose, from many, one to guide my stanzas.
I see a free-born State, still free indeed,
By thrift and temperance gaining the lead;
Stand forth amid thy golden sheaves, fair Kansas.

—E. P. Chittenden.

"AD·ASTRA PER ASPERA."

Beautiful Kansas, whose glory and fame
Thy children in song and story proclaim;
Though born in battle and baptized in blood,
Thou art the home of the noble and good;
And thy sons and daughters shall grandly rise
Through difficulties to the starry skies.

—R. L. Cochran.

Not for what she has done for me,
Though it be great,
For what she is, her majesty,
I love my State.

—Thomas Emmet Dewey.

THE blazing star upon our checkered page,
The pavement where the foot of Liberty
Rests firm—the gem of all our boasted age
And land, burns brightest in the galaxy
Of stars, which represents our claim
To Freedom's best and sweetest name.

—*Jas. A. DeMoss.*

WHEN Freedom's banner is unfurled,
No star among its folds of blue
Shines forth to nations far and wide
With luster brighter, with beams more true;
Though oft mid clouds 't is hidden quite,
It rises ever for the right.

—*Ida Capen Fleming.*

MY Kansas! your praises I would sing,
Dear State of progress, peace, and plenty, all combined.
Spring, Summer, Autumn yield their golden stores,
And some new joys in Winter hours we find:
Then Christmas crowns our land with cheer,
And warms our hearts throughout the year.

—*Ad. H. Gibson.*

THE land of blizzards, cyclones, coyotes and humanity; therefore, the land of the free and the home of the brave.

—*Richard S. Graves.*

KANSAS HEROES.

NOT best the stretching fields of golden grain,
The harvest plentitude of fertile plain;
'T was not for these they struck the effectual blow
That broke the power of a malignant foe.
Their blood for Freedom shed must consecrate
To human Liberty this sovereign State.

—*Allen D. Gray.*

SHE came a child, homeless, forlorn;
She wandered wild the prairies over,
Nurtured by tossing winds; one morn
She rose a goddess with a lover.
A loving people kneel to praise
"Through hope to stars!" the song they raise.

—*Mary T. Gray.*

KANSAS is Freedom's birthplace, glory's pathway, chivalry's temple, the home of patriotism. A land whose boundless plains and deathless waters have witnessed the dawn of fame. —*Lizzie B. Hamrick.*

ABOVE CRITICISM.

MY love, much praised, much blamed, grows moody quite,
The good words fail to drive away the ill;
But Kansas, blessed, maligned, shows no affright;
Instead, moves nobly on, unruffled still;
Serenely sure, unminding wreaths of scars,
Firm-stepped, she mounts her pathway to the stars.

—*Chas. Moreau Harger.*

KANSAS! Home of the fair and free,
Accept the greeting of thy devotee.
Noblest of republics, beauteous, land,
Shatterer of chains, strong to command,
All hail! Uncounted millions look to thee,
Sovereign of freedom, truth and purity.

—*Clara H. Hazelrigg.*

A NEW army in emotional Kansas carries plow handles for rifles, turns the school houses into forts, votes for reform, and takes offices by storm. —*Ewing Herbert.*

AS KNIGHT of old, alone, before the fray,
Rode out to meet his boldest foe midway,
Met, strove and conquered in the army's sight,
And came with trophy worthy of the fight:
So thou, my State, return, thy Leader greet,
And lay a broken wine glass at His feet.

—*Hattie Horner.*

A GODDESS born of hero pains, free, wise,
Full armored. With the war cry "*Ad Astra per Aspera*"
On her lips, she bounded into Statehood!
Her most loyal son, Governor John A. Martin,
Fitted this legend of Minerva's birth to Kansas:
Never fitter simile nor more fit eulogist.

—*Mrs. J. K. Hudson.*

In eighteen hundred sixty-one, when manly cheeks turned pale,
To give thee Freedom's glorious birth our Nation did travail.
Four hundred by two hundred miles thy fertile, rolling plain;
More than a million outstretched hands to glean thy golden grain;
Eight thousand and nine hundred schools, where knowledge we acquire;
Three thousand forty churches call: "O Kansas, look up higher!"

—*Tirzah A. Hoyland.*

— —

Fair, sunny State! Endowed at birth
With attributes of sterling worth,
Enthusiasm, loyalty to right,
Courage and zeal to cope with might,
Baptized in blood, her nature still
To down the wrong with sovereign will.

—*Mary A. Humphrey.*

— —

THE THIRTY-FOURTH STAR.

Amidst the gathering gloom, around our Nation's flag,
There arose its fairest star above the sea of wrong,
A brilliant, radiant gem that shall forever shine,
The brightest diadem among the starry throng,
And in its upward course to freedom and to right,
E'en nations turn to watch its glorious flight.

—*Mary E. Jackson.*

AN ACROSTIC.

Kansas! Fair State, we well may claim
  A meed of praise for thee;
None other boasts so great a fame,
  So grand a history,
As through oppressions, strifes and wars
She soars triumphant to the stars.

—*Maggie Kilmer.*

Full thirty years I've known thee,
  Thou land of wondrous growing;
Choicest center from the sea,
  Thy great wealth outward flowing,
Fills the earth with happiness,
  While untold more we're showing.
Shall we pride in thee confess?
  Yea: swear eternal loving.

—*Sam. Kimble.*

Here first my boyhood days were passed
  Beneath the sunflower's cluster;
Let strangers chide her if they will,
  I surely still shall trust her.
Let ingrates wander far and wide,
  From Madrin to Matanzas,
But win or lose, I'll stand my hand,
  For aye in bonnie Kansas.

The wretched slave, whose galling chains the gods
  Dared not to break, turned in his mute despair
To Kansas, and she struck for him a blow
  That swelled into a universal prayer,
Till o'er the tomb of Slavery rose the star
Of Freedom, shining through the clouds of war!

—Will. Lisenbee.

Kansas, like thy favorite flower,
  Has thy race, thus far, been run;
Morning, evening, finds thee facing
  Towards the right's progressive sun.

—Sol. T. Long.

One is at times tempted to call Kansas, "Dryasdust!" At any rate, like that worthy, she has introduced to the world some notable personages. *—Mrs. E. S. E. Loomis.*

KANSAS IN SIX VERSES.

The State where sudden Death on Hope advances,
And Faith in rains and crops hops all the chances;
Where Politics is pierced with lunging lances,
As forth to vote the frisky Farmer prances;
Where now the "Money Bug" withdraws his glances,
And leaves the Wind to funny, sunny Kansas.

—Joel Moody.

IF all the States were stars
And woven in a crown,
And as a mark of excellence
On Nature's brow were bound,
Kansas with a radiance bright
Would from the very topmost height
Eclipse the light of all.

—W. A. McCausland.

OLD Sol, from his majestic height,
While viewing States, was asked to choose
That one where man could happiest dwell.
He scanned them well, than stopped to muse,
When Kansas passing—"There!" he cried,
"Choose Kansas and you'll nothing lose."

—"Monnie Moore."

SON, you are in Kansas and literature, the best State and vocation in the wide world. If still unsatisfied, what do you want—the earth? *—Tom. P. Morgan.*

KANSAS, how sublime thy story,
Crowning of a nation's glory;
First in all our hearts forever;
First the slave's cursed bonds to sever;
With thy temperance banner o'er us,
Bright the future's sheen before us.

—Laura E. Newell.

Drenched with impetuous martyr blood she stands,
A nation's pride — the weeping cynosure
Of all the world. Deflowered by ruthless hands,
Defamed, dishonored, 'reft of all that 's pure,
To rise a spotless monument, at last,
For all the future and to all the past.

— *Albert Bigelow Paine.*

Sing a song for Kansas! be sure to boil it down;
I know the happy sunflower maid is sometimes known to frown;
She goes for prohibition, and goes for Ingalls, too:
Without her lengthy senator, what would poor Kansas do?
She owns a small Alliance, but it has n't come to stay;
I 'll tell you more about it some other sunny day.

— *Ellen Patton.*

Child of the grassy plain,
Facing the day,
Blooming in sun or rain,
Evermore gay,
Coming the first to bless
Wide-spreading wilderness,
Flaunting and free,
Coming in power,
Kansas is like to thee,
Sunflower.

— *Noble L. Prentis.*

I HAVE known Kansas thirty-one years, as a Territory and as a State, in war and in peace, in famine and in plenty, and I have never known a man who trusted and believed in her, and in evil times waited and hoped for better, who was disappointed or deceived. Those who have known Kansas longest love her most. —*Caroline E. Prentis.*

KANSAS is the Nation's political experiment farm. Reforms admitted to be desirable, but of doubtful practicability, are first tried in Kansas. If they fail here, the experiment is carried no farther. —*Chas. F. Scott.*

PAUPER or king—as up and down swift slips
The mercury of chance. Or, bud to rose,
And then a withered stem, all in a day!
Is 't strange, when empty-pursed and petal bare,
We love thee most? For, without warning note,
In walks the king; the bush is full of blooms!

—*W. H. Simpson.*

KISMET.

A WORD doth make our destiny. We bravely said
Ad astra, when the night engulfed our martyred dead;
And when the morning flushed the pallid eastern sky,
Our chosen character was registered on high.

—*Florence L. Snow.*

Thine is the land where the swift flying shadows
Wander at will o'er monotonous plains;
Kiss the fresh blossoms that spangle the meadows
And sail o'er seas of voluptuous grains.
Dear are thy chidings and sweet thy caresses,
Tender thy eyes where the warm lovelight broods;
Bright is the sunlight amid thy soft tresses,
Loving thy heart, but inconstant thy moods.

— *Geo. C. Sperry.*

— —

I love thee, home land, when I pass
In western wilds, through wind-tossed grass;
And yet more dearly when I spy
Thy rosy children romping by;
But yet of all I count this best—
Thy moral honor, east and west.

— *Mrs. L. E. Thrope.*

— —

KANSAS—THERE SHE STANDS.

Out of a motionless ocean of sand,
Whose petrified billows stretched far to the west,
Kansas sprang up like an enchanted land,
With wealth more than many a king can command,
Where civilization's first favors expand,
Pork packers, pap, passes and poets on hand—
Who says that our State is not wondrously blessed?

—*Will. A. White.*

Of all the States, but three shall live in story:
  Old Massachusetts with her Plymouth Rock,
  And old Virginia with her noble stock,
And sunny Kansas with her woes and glory;
These three will live in song and oratory.
  While all the others with their idle claims
  Will only be remembered as mere names.

—*E. F. Ware.*

The most remarkable thing about Kansas, from '54 to '91, has been its courage and moral leadership. —*D. W. Wilder.*

www.ingramcontent.com/pod-product-compliance
Lightning Source LLC
Chambersburg PA
CBHW020548270326
41927CB00006B/763

* 9 7 8 3 3 3 7 2 1 7 9 6 9 *